What to Expect
from College

What to Expect
from College

A University President's Guide
for Students and Parents

George Dennis O'Brien

ST. MARTIN'S PRESS   NEW YORK

DESIGN BY JUDITH A. STAGNITTO

Library of Congress Cataloging-in-Publication Data

O'Brien, George Dennis
        What to expect from college : a university president's guide for students and parents / George Dennis O'Brien.
                p.   cm.
        "A Thomas Dunne book."
        Includes index.
        ISBN 0-312-06436-5
        1. College student orientation—United States.
        I. Title.
        LB2343.32.O27   1991   91-19077
        378.1'98—dc20   CIP

First Edition: September 1991
10 9 8 7 6 5 4 3 2 1

Dedicated to my children
Elizabeth
Juliana
Victoria
and the colleges of their choice

Contents

Advice to the Reader

Who should read this book? Anyone trying to understand the modern collegiate and university world. The *special* audience intended is applicants and parents who are mulling over guidebooks and individual college promotional material. In those handy handbooks and glossy pamphlets, the reader will be enticed by a variety of claims and charmed by magic terms. "Rustic College believes in teaching!" "Megastate University affirms the liberal arts." Is there a difference between colleges and universities? Are there some wretched institutions which do *not* believe in teaching? What *exactly* are the liberal arts, anyhow—and would it matter if one knew?

College may be the most under-informed important life choice. This may seem surprising given the deluge of facts and statistics so earnestly compiled in the many published guides. But the facts may present themselves—all too frequently *do* present themselves—as obscure clues to a mystery plot yet to be revealed. This book aims to reveal the basic *plot*. What is college all about?

The answer to that question is far from clear. Despite all the high rhetoric of admissions pamphlets and presidential addresses—I have delivered plenty myself—it seems clear that the *modern* university remains a mystery. Proof? I cite early on a researcher who notes that students across the country seem to have no "fun" at college. Then, fewer and fewer seek advanced degrees: having tasted academia for four years they hasten to go elsewhere. Funlessness and flight from academia suggest to me that the higher education message has been garbled. I believe that students should find their undergraduate years fulfilling (maybe even "fun") and that more should choose to keep right on through advanced study. Perhaps if the mystery of college were fully unveiled, students would appreciate its true reward.

The book is divided into two sections. The first section attempts to characterize the modernity of American colleges and universities. Under all the Gothic façades, behind the mottos of Puritan founders, lies a remarkable modern invention: the American university. By tracing its history, I hope to reveal its essence. The second section assumes the basic story of modernity and turns to a series of specific issues that concern the collegiate consumer and the general public beyond.

Thus, to applicants and parents about to make the plunge into collegiate mystery, I offer a key for understanding. Understanding college before choosing one will make the journey more fulfilling. If this treatment illuminates policy makers and the general public, I will also be pleased. I even hope that for my colleagues inside the ivy walls, self-understanding will improve our practice.

PART 1

Myths

I'm having no fun"—the opening student comment in Helen Horowitz's 1987 account of contemporary college life, *Campus Life*. What else is new? Was college *ever* fun? Old-time Yalies might sing, "Bright college life with pleasures rife / The shortest, gladdest years of life"—but was it so? In the nineteenth century student riots were epidemic at the nation's colleges as young people protested academic sterility, boredom, moral restraint, poor food, and cold lodgings. In the late twentieth century moral restraint seems to have vanished along with starched collars, the curriculum is trendy, and universities spend megadollars entertaining youth with everything from rock concerts to football extravaganzas. And still it's no fun?

Horowitz claims that funlessness is widespread. There is that in the nature of the modern college which seems to check the cheerful. To be precise, adolescent college *years* may be "pleasure rife," but the pleasure is likely to be extracurricular. The modern college week is five days of "work" and a weekend for "partying." That classes and fun are split seems to me an all too doleful conclusion about colleges and universities. The split may not even be real. (Though it is fashionable talk in most student centers. An anthropologist who recently surveyed the campus scene notes that students frequently speak a foreign language that he calls Undergraduate Cynical.)

This book is intended to diagnose and relieve (if possible) depression on the campus quad. There is much to fume about on any academic quad: racial discrimination, lack of updated facilities, vanishing faculty, incoherent curricula. Food is more plentiful than a century ago, but it is still institutional hash. Nevertheless, college is a better deal and "funner" (my daughters' contribution to English lexicography) than one might suspect when hearing Undergraduate Cynical.

On the other hand, I do not intend that this book should offer President Pollyanna's pleasant platitudes on collegiate life. The modern university is an unusual social invention; it has existed in its current form for slightly more than a century and its American form is different in important ways from any other universities world wide. If students, parents, senators, and a noted secretary of education find themselves dismayed at the whole business of higher education, it is frequently because they have a different collegiate story line than the one currently being run through everywhere from Harvard to the University of Texas at the Permian Basin. A very broad formulation of that discrepancy would characterize it as the clash between "collegiate myth" and "university reality." The discrepancy is in some measure the result of a time lag. The myth of the college (with pleasures rife) that is held up to the grimsville classroom of the modern university, is in part the application of nineteenth-century spiritual aspiration to twentieth-century academic fact.

My hope in this book is to give some broad description of the modern university for students, parents, and a variety of anxious observers of the scholarly scenery. The intent is not merely academic. If parents are to spend sixty thousand dollars plus on private higher education, if taxpayers are asked to build three more state universities, if students are to suffer through elementary calculus, it would be well for each and all to have some understanding of the governing idea of the whole academic show. I believe that most are following the wrong myth. The persistence of "the collegiate myth" is not surprising. It has been and still is very attractive—and, besides, it is the not-so-subtle image conveyed in every college admissions brochure.

Once (for my venial sins) I spent a whole day looking at various college promotional films. As the last sunset set over the last college chapel-on-the-hill and the last quartet warbled the last chords of the last local Unique College song, it struck me that everyone was selling nineteenth-century sentiment—not twentieth-century education. If you start off for a Victorian carpet dance and end up at a lecture on the Krebs cycle, you're likely to register some level of disappointment.

I have divided my diagnosis of Contemporary College into two sections. The first I have entitled "Myths." In part I am concerned with *false* images, but I am really more interested in *myth as basic story*. The old-time college—sentimentally packaged in the promo film—and the modern university—experienced at exam time—both have a prevailing story line, an institutionial mythos that gives point and perspective to the bits and pieces. My aim in the first section is to give some notion of the modern mythos of higher education. Perhaps if one understands what to expect from college it will be more satisfying—even if it doesn't quite hit the fun button.

The second section is entitled "Facts." Here I take up a variety of dicey items in college life as they may influence student, parent, taxpayer, or talk-show host in appraising higher ed. I begin by reviewing guidebooks. This is not a quidebook, but it might be thought of as a guide to guidebooks. A guidebook may correctly tell one that Old Nostalgia is a "liberal arts" college. We know from consumer demand that "liberal arts" is a pro-term. But what (if anything) does it mean? My hope is to give some reality to this and other rhetorical flourishes of collegiate promotion.

Similar mysteries surround other high-flying terms: "university" or "college," "public" or "private," "vocational" or "general" education. All of the above are hung out as enticements for consumers, but their lure is inversely proportional to their comprehensibility. Having probed the simple mysteries that distinguish colleges and universities (is one such mystery spelling, perhaps?), I turn to absolute mysteries like sex and the single student, fraternities, and football. In the hope that all the revelations attempted, higher education looks attractive, I discuss admissions and paying for it all in tuition and taxes.

Who should read this account of college? I recommend it especially to parents whose children are about to be or are currently enmeshed in education beyond high school. Understanding teens is difficult enough; understanding the social institutions of teendom (college being one) should not compound bafflement. This is not a Dr. Spock book for parenting children in college. Rather, I am concerned that as the generations of mankind and academia have plodded on, something strange and different has happened to "going to college." Critics and consumers of colleges should have some sense of the ultramodern institution hidden behind all those crumbling Gothic façades. The modern university is one of the culture's greatest inventions. What most people don't realize is the sheer novelty of the thing. Like all modern inventions the university has it vices, and they will be detailed; but it is best to appraise universities and automobiles for what they are: not classrooms without monks or carriages that lack horses. Understanding what a university is may not increase the fun to joy overflowing, but it could direct grumbling to the right issues.

1

Bullish on Bachelor's Degrees

I s college worth the consumer's cost? If the intent of this text is to drive out depression, it might as well start with a really fun issue. Few items are as likely to stir bile as the bursar's bill. Even students at state institutions face tuition charges and a host of fees; their parents mull tax increases for the benefit of higher ed. There is no way to demonstrate cost and benefit if one is mistaken about the benefit. Believe a false myth about college benefit and you will be disappointed in the actual results. Since cost is such a complex matter, it gets a whole chapter later in this book. But without a preliminary overview of dollars spent and desires met, the average reader will quit right now—adding the cost of this book to the escalating price spiral of higher education.

If you calculate lost earnings during college years and balance that against the difference in lifetime income of college graduates and high-school graduates you will get an argument. *The Case Against College,* a recent popular book by Caroline Bird, showed with impressive statistics that—overall and in the long run and making a few assumptions and so on—college education just does not turn out to be a good financial deal. You do *not* earn more money as a result of your college education. There must be something to this thesis, since Ms. B. has been earning a very handsome living lecturing on her view at college campuses across the country.

On the other hand, numerous studies with various other calculations show that the average life earnings of the college graduate are considerably in excess of those of his or her high-school peer. I am inclined to believe the latter statistics, not only because they help justify *my* life choice as a university president but because I have never met a brain surgeon who had only a high-school education.

There was a time when economic statistics would have been decisive. In the nineteenth century, when a significant number of college graduates entered the Christian ministry, one would surely not have chosen college as a career path to wealth—at least not wealth in this world. By contrast, in the first fifty years of the twentieth century any old college education would have been a reasonable guarantee of status or economic advancement. Before World War II, less than 6 percent of the U.S. population had a college degree. College graduates were a rare enough commodity to have assured entry into a variety of white-collar and protoprofessional jobs. Pay was usually better than average and—as they say—"no heavy lifting." Current complaints about the economic value of a bachelor's degree stem in part from the expansion of bachelors on the market. As supply increases to meet (or exceed) demand, the price that a college degree commands in the market will fall (Economics 101).

If any old B.A. won't automatically underwrite an invitation to the country club, buyers become leery, wary, and choosy. If I don't make it to Prestige U and I will have to take the bank training program anyhow, why not plunge into the market right away and avoid compulsory French?

Though upward economic mobility cannot be guaranteed by an up-to-date diploma, still the odds are better with the diploma than without it. One of the most lucrative careers in America is professional sports. One can obviously succeed as an athlete without the benefit of a college education; recent athletic scandals suggest that a number of graduates have done just that. Nevertheless, a reasonable calculation would suggest that a youngster from Harlem has a much better chance of entering the ABA (American Bar Association) than playing in the NBA.

The reason for the better odds on law is the underlying trend toward professionalization in American society. Everything from brain surgery to basket weaving apparently demands specialized training these days. Professionalization of careers rests on the supposition that for each career there exists a body of formally teachable—and needed—skill. Colleges and universities will give (they actually "sell") specialized knowledge about neurons or Lotus 1-2-3. The days of flying by the seat of the pants out of the school of hard knocks into the rat race are rapidly vanishing into the American career sunset. As American society has become more broadly and hierarchically professionalized, advanced education of some form emerges as virtually the only pathway to a credentialed career.

College education may not be for those who thrive on high risk. Movie stardom, a killing at the casino, and a bonus from the Red Sox yield handsome rewards and are infinitely more glamorous than a career in cost accounting. But if you choose to be schooled in cost accounting you will have a reasonably predictable path toward a job. Spectacular exceptions aside, it is more and more true that advanced schooling is the only way toward jobs that cannot be replaced by a bar-code reader.

"College for career" *should* be the basic economic argument for higher education, and it is an argument widely advertised. I have made such speeches myself. But for all the practical career talk about colleges, the reality of college is strangely different. As a sometime professor of *philosophy* (and most-of-the-time university president) I should certainly wonder what Immanuel Kant has to do with careers. By the logic of financial success, colleges and universities should be through-and-through professional training camps. But they usually aren't; even the professional-training-camp colleges cannot quite bear to admit what they are. Yes, college is the key to a career, but each and every college and university, however lofty or lowly, promises something *more.* The "more" is the essence of higher ed and the reason why one chooses old Siwash over Southern Tech. What is the "more"?

If the commercial justification for education is professional training, one would expect American colleges and universities to become strictly professional-training schools. At least in fact—if not in admissions advertising—the rush to career training is evident throughout higher education. I recently attended a graduation at a small liberal-arts college and scanned the degrees. One would have expected history majors and English degrees galore. They were few. Most were in straight job-related fields: accounting, communication arts, marketing, and so on. Business dominated the bachelor's degrees.

Examining the degree distribution at even our most traditional universities and colleges, one sees flight to what would appear to be a first approximation of career-oriented curricula. I recall Yale's President, Kingman Brewster, inveighing many years ago about the fact that half of the entering class at Yale claimed to be pre-med. The world did not need that many Yale doctors. Today the trend is economics, which sounds like the next best thing to a present seat on the stock exchange.

Professional training in higher education is here to stay and it is antiquarian elitism to pretend otherwise. Universities and colleges might as well be straightforward about promoting the professional and career interests of their students. The *mystery* about higher education in the United States on the edge of the twenty-first century is that it exhibits such a high resistance in rhetoric, reality, and degree requirements to careerism in the curriculum. To understand the American college experience, one has to assess the basic aspiration to "the liberal arts," "general education," and all that is *non*specialized and *non*-careerist. The economic argument for college is clear enough if students buy COBOL for their educational dollar: Then they can talk to the company computer. But even the most tech-y institute will suggest that its real aim is something infinitely more worthy than mere skill: the "higher" learning. The higher the learning, the higher the cost of production—and sometimes the price to the consumer.

To understand the strange romance of American higher education with the elevated and elusive world beyond mere career, I will tell two stories, both true. The moral of the stories is paradoxical, since they prove that utterly practical education is impractical—and worse yet, maybe, un-American.

At a meeting of the Cabinet of President John Adams in 1794, the distinguished secretaries were presented with a table full of musket parts. They were then invited by the manufacturer of these bits and pieces, Mr. Eli Whitney, to try their hands at a do-it-yourself musket. They did so with considerable success; the Secretary of State, Thomas Jefferson, noted the event in his diary. Americans have been do-it-yourself types from that day to the latest Sears Roebuck instructions for the family lawn mower. ("Put hex nut 6 in slot A and turn . . .")

The event in President Adams's Cabinet office was extraordinarily significant and emblematic of something distinctly American. Whitney illustrated what we now call the principle of interchangeable parts but which was referred to in the nineteenth century as "the American system." Before Whitney's inspiration about matched manufactured musket parts, muskets were a craftsman's product, individually tooled and incomparable one unto the other. Musket making was a specialized art well beyond even the learning of Thomas Jefferson. That a group of politicians could assemble a weapon was miraculous.

The deep significance of the American system was the relation which it signified between worker and skill. In the Old World workers were specialized; in the New World machines were specialized and workers were generalists. Making was not a secret of guarded crafts, trades, or guilds. The American system is a continuing cultural truth, and it applies particularly to the sense and meaning of higher education. European higher education retains an air of the craft tradition. One chooses a specialized faculty on entrance to the university. The American higher education, for all that it has taken from the Germans (of which much more later), retains the American system of generalist education.

A handbook on the modern American university must begin, therefore, with the generalist as the basic "product" of college experience. What is one supposed to get from higher learning in the United States? Not a specialized career, but something infinitely more fuzzy. Why finance fuzziness?

Simple job-oriented-professional-careerism may be un-American if the example of Eli Whitney and the muskets holds. Bad enough for career education that it is unpatriotic; there is a better argument that some degree of impracticalness is best for the practical life. If, in the most prestigious groves of academe, professionalism always yields to some ancestral specter of the liberal arts, it is because of a wispy belief that "liberal arts" make professions fertile. I prove it with a Harvard fertility myth—and also a true story.

My tale is recounted by Bill Perry, long-time head of the Bureau of Study Counsel at Harvard. The story is true but names have been changed to protect the innocent, assuming that there are any at Harvard. It seems that a student called Metzger was scheduled to meet a chum at the Loeb Theater after a rehearsal. As it happened, Metzger had mistaken the day and arrived not after a rehearsal but just as a class was filing in for an examination. Having already missed his appointment, Metzger decided for a lark to take the test, which was in a subject Metzger had never studied. Nevertheless, he scribbled answers furiously and signed the paper, with a flourish, "Smith."

As good luck—for tale tellers—would have it, there was a Smith in the class and he was ill on that day. Metzger-Smith's exam went through the works and was returned with an A. This was too-good news to keep in the rumor mill; the whole sordid tale was published with glee in the *Crimson*. Naturally Metzger-Smith was in trouble—Harvard has a rule against taking exams you aren't supposed to. But the one in real difficulty was the instructor who had given the A. Didn't that prove the invalidity of grading?

Bill Perry was a friend of both Metzger and the instructor. He decided after investigating the facts that the grade was perfectly justified and wrote a most perceptive essay to prove his point. The course in question was in anthropology. The question on the examination involved writing a book review of one of two assigned books. Metzger, of course, had read neither. The one he chose to review was *The American Character*, by Geoffrey Gorer. Now, while Mr. Metzger had never taken any anthropology, he had sat at enough dinner-table conversations at Eliot House, one of Harvard's many small residential units, to be quite familiar with the problem of cultural relativism: People tend to speak not only fact but their own perception of fact. Metzger judged that Geoffrey Gorer was an Anglo-Saxon type, so he wrote a splendid essay on the problems of observing the American character from within a set of already given cultural assumptions. He ended the essay with true chutzpah: "And so this book tells us as much about Geoffrey Gorer as about the American character."

Perry argued that Metzger had accomplished a rare feat in academia. He had produced an essay of pure bull. Unfortunately, most essays are contaminated by some shreds of fact, but Metger's exam was one hundred percent and Grade A. For Perry, bull is much closer to the essence of higher education than the usual earnest effort of examination writers. He defines bull as follows:

> To bull: to discourse on the principles, contexts, and methods which would give understanding, meaning, and perspective to facts or data with the intent of deceiving the reader into believing that you have such facts or data—which of course you do not.

Bull is of course a well-known academic species, though it is seldom as elegantly defined. Unfortunately, we fail to appreciate its virtue because we lack recognition and definition of its opposite, which is—naturally—"cow."

> To cow: to give facts and data without any discourse on the principles, contexts, and methods which would give understanding, meaning, and perspective to such facts or data with the intent of deceiving the reader into believing that you really understand what you are talking about—which of course you do not.

Perry argues that bull is much closer to real education than cow is. Most of what is received in examinations is well-meaning cow. Of course, the ideal for education is the happy marriage of bull and cow, but ultimately the bull is more valuable. (No sexist overtones intended.)

The bull's transcendental quality is the measure of the best education. Bull is the heart of the "liberal-arts" overlay of the most prestigious college or university. The aim of every subject—even economics—is to teach not fact and data but principle and method. The real lesson is being able to discover the context that will give meaning and understanding to data. Unless the student discovers that context, the result will be cow, and usually incoherent cow. (Bad writing = straight cow.)

It may seem that the Metzger case is stacked from the start by the fact that the exam was in a "humanistic" subject like anthropology. Here is a similar story from the sciences. (This one is too good to be true. But it works.) Again the student is set an exam question. This time he flunks but protests to the dean that the grade is totally unfair. The dean reluctantly agrees and the faculty member is willing to set another exam. The question is: How do you determine the height of a tower with a barometer? The student sits and fiddles for most of the time allotted and finally scribbles down an answer. The instructor gives him an A but asks why he spent so long before writing. The student replies that there were so many answers he was trying to figure out which one to give. What other answers?

"Well," the student says, "one could measure the height of the barometer and its shadow, then measure the length of the tower's shadow and calculate the height. Or, one could go to the top of the tower and throw off the barometer and time its fall. By the formula for acceleration of bodies one could decide the height of the tower. Or, one could measure the tower in barometer lengths. If all else failed, you could go to the watchman and say, 'Here, I have this valuable barometer. I will give it to you if you will tell me the height of the tower.' "

Nils Bohr once said to an associate: "That idea is crazy, but not crazy enough to be true." The trouble with "professional" education without the spirit of "liberal arts" is that one gets facts that are not crazy enough to be true. In the long run, the lack of a liberal perspective diminishes the value of the professional education. The reason is very simple: One never enters the profession where one hopes to leave it. Too much so-called professional education (and student interest) is concentrated on the entry point, where present fact milked from the cow of the current curriculum will serve. The question for career is whether one can bull one's way into the next job— where you may know as little as Mr. Metzger did on the fatal afternoon at Loeb Theater. For people without a sense of first principles, first jobs in any profession become last jobs as well.

Various studies show that the great discoveries in science have frequently been made by individuals who were not specialists in the area of discovery. It is alleged that one of the reasons mathematicians tend to make their great discoveries when they are young is that they are too inexperienced to realize that the problem cannot be solved in the way that they have, in fact, solved it. Too much sheer careerism in calculus and commerce precludes the inventor and the entrepreneur.

In the spirit of Mr. Metzger's enlightening example, this small volume wishes to distinguish itself both from admissions advertising and guidebook compendia. Much of the latter is sheer cow—facts without meaning; much of the former is bad bull—elegant generality without even inner coherence. My aim is to marry bull and cow, meaning and fact, but with the emphasis on meaning. The best education *is* bull.

2

President (and Parent):
A Qualified Role

My first administrative position in higher education was dean of dropouts. That was not the official title—which was "Assistant Dean of the College" (at Princeton)—but it came to be my preferred description of the daily duties. It was the responsibility of this lowly office to deal with all failures, withdrawals, leaves, or other mysterious absences from the university. I was the *de*-admissions officer. There is nothing like *de*-admitting fifty talented teenagers a term from one of America's great universities to set the mind to wondering what colleges and their inhabitants mean to one another.

That anyone would leave Princeton for any cause whatsoever other than death was baffling to veteran Princetonians. Failures could hardly be explained by incompetence, since this highly selective student body displayed the most impressive of academic credentials. Voluntary departure because of dissatisfaction was regarded by loyalist Tigers as akin to voluntary withdrawal from heaven.

Sitting day after day with disaster cases was an early lesson in the rationality (or lack of it) of the collegiate experience. My favorite example of "irrational" appraisal was also the most frequent. The most-often-repeated complaint against 1960s Princeton: "There are no women here." (A fault since repaired.) My kindly reply was standard: "Well, that can't have come as a surprise. You certainly knew when you were admitted that this was an all-male institution." Sophomore: "Yes, sir, but it didn't seem to be so important then!"

I leave it to the reader to decide how rational it is to evaluate a college because of the prevailing sex distribution—but it is surely done. I would list this choice as romantic in contrast to the presumably rational grounds for assessing college excellence: the strength of the faculty, the size of the library, the quality (not the gender) of the student body. (A *rational* choice along gender lines might be the all-women's colleges. There is a strong educational argument that women perform better in single-sex collegiate settings.) The problem with rationality is as the great Pascal noted: The heart (yea, even or especially the sophomore heart) hath its reasons which the reasonable dean knoweth not.

If the sophomore breast seeks romance, I discovered as dean of dropouts that parents had a different rationale about junior staying in college. Invariably the parent of the designated flunk-out would appear in my office to plead for restoration of the offspring. They weren't much interested in the gender issue. They wanted this progeny to succeed and they often would berate the dreary student for wasting all that tuition money. (Flunking out does not yield refunds. President Hibben of Princeton was supposed to have said to a perturbed parent: "If you are in any way dissatisfied, we return the boy!")

Parental interest in money well spent, and student interest in the other things of life do not always mesh. When I was at Middlebury College in the 1960s we had a very with-it public-relations director who proposed to bring out an admissions brochure modeled on the *Whole Earth Catalogue*. This compendium of environmental piety and exotic lore was published in large format on newsprint and was a definite best-seller with everybody's applicant pool. The PR officer obviously thought that Middlebury could be well advertised in that style. I objected: "Since the parents are paying six thousand dollars for a college education (this was the late 1960s) they want something that looks like an IBM debenture."

Given the clash between parental financial prudence and student fascinations, it is a wonder that parents seem to be so little involved in collegiate choice. This chapter has the title it does because, as president and parent I want to qualify on two scores to comment on colleges. The interesting fact is that parents so often retreat from the college process, aside from driving applicants on the grand tour, paying the bills, and beaming at the commencement ceremony. My intention is to qualify both the author and any "senior" reader to speak with some modest authority about universities and colleges. That is not easy, and a parental reader may feel more out of it than a presidential author.

The ambitious Middlebury PR person who wanted to sell college like the whole earth was in tune with what many believe is current family ideology. One often hears the claim that Jim or Jane solo chose the college he or she wanted to attend. Can this be the whole truth? There is some interesting cultural history that explains such a declaration of applicant independence.

If one takes a historical glance at families over the last century, one finds that there has been a remarkable reversal of relations between parents and their adolescent children. In the nineteenth century, children of "college" age (not that many of that age group went to college) were almost always *financially* independent of their parents, but remained *spiritually* dependent. An eighteen-year-old in the 1880s was most likely to be married and supporting children. At the same time we have ample records of children continuing to seek moral and spiritual guidance from parents on through the lifetime of the older generation. Middle-aged males would write long letters to Father seeking moral counsel on some life decision, and expect wisdom to flow down the family line.

By the end of the twentieth century this pattern often appears in reverse. The adolescent (or older) child is likely to be *economically* dependent, but to have been *spiritually* independent since the day when he or she discovered heavy metal, Sinead O'Connor, and the Grateful Dead. The modern invention of "youth" creates a novel claim of spiritual status and independence—of which more in a later chapter. The notion that young people alone pick their colleges is part of an ambient American family ethic.

Families are, however, hardier and more complex than pop culture might allow. To be sure, one is not likely to utter "Yale" or "State" in the sepulchral tones of ripe Victorian parenting and expect instant adolescent acquiescence. The discourse is more subtle. Most parents manage to sketch a short list (usually with special guest starters from the applicant). *The* college will be chosen from *the* list. The aim of every ambitious college admissions officer is to make the parental short list.

I offer testimony from personal history of the value of parental power. I cannot actually recall applying to college—at least not in what anyone would have regarded as an active mode. Although I must have assumed that I would go on to something after high school, I was extremely apprehensive of more and more and more schooling, which did seem to be both long and tedious. My mother did all the work (Father being away at the war). She sent for a catalogue from every college on the East Coast from Dartmouth to Duke. I read none of them. Nothing is more boring for after-solid-geometry casual reading than a college catalogue. (These were the days before admissions brochures discovered Kodachrome.) I finally *had* to apply to something so I chose the college that sent the most charming cover letter. As luck would have it, that was Yale, and as even more luck would have it, they accepted me. So much for rational decision making!

My own youngest daughter recently went through the admissions process. Of course, we followed the advice of this book and insinuated a short list of worthy suggestions. She in turn foraged on her own, and the results suggested that applicant wisdom has not grown since my own efforts—or lack thereof—forty years ago. The first college catalogue she solicited on her own turned out to be from "another college by the same name" in a part of the geographical and spiritual universe remote from her known actual preferences. I called my mother for help.

One of the hopes of this book is to assist any other mother out there who wants to create a list. My mother may not have been wholly rational in choosing "Eastern colleges" to generate the Dartmouth-to-Duke array, but there are lots of excellent institutions along the Atlantic. There are, however, more fine-tuned principles for creating a rational list than propinquity to large oceans. To assist in Mom's little list, I hope to sketch the plot and characters of the academic drama, and then fill in the scenary and minor characters.

To encourage parents to enter into college assessing with tentative audacity, let me now say that becoming a practiced collegiate appraiser is decidedly difficult. Although I offer this book as aid and comfort, I confess considerable hesitation about my own competency. (One of the virtues of this treatment may be to make the reader wary of any and all who pretend to make judgments about the character and quality of colleges.) Knowing the character of a college is no less mysterious than determining the character of the potential applicant. I do not need to remind most modern parents about the mysteries of their own offspring. If it is often difficult to understand Johnny, who is underfoot most of the time, consider how difficult it is to know Winsocki from its admissions brochure.

Despite the general warning, I have learned something more about colleges and universities since I picked Yale because of the warmth of its bureaucratic prose. My own educational and professional experience has been moderately extended—English at Yale, philosophy graduate work at the University of Chicago, faculty service at Princeton, Middlebury College, Bucknell University, and the University of Rochester. I have taught part-time at Rutgers and La Salle College (now University) in Philadelphia. I have held various administrative responsibilities for more than thirty years. In addition to being "dean of dropouts" I have been a dean of men, dean of the college, and dean of the faculty. (For a time I held both the latter positions simultaneously and was referred to in the student newspaper as "Dean of the World." It remains my favorite title.) At Bucknell and Rochester I have been president, while continuing to teach at least one course a year for the sake of sanity.

Thirty years of experience in university teaching and administration certainly should give one some experience about the character and range of American higher education. On the other hand, a knowledgeable observer will have noted that this is a rather rarefied list of institutions. It contains several of the country's greatest universities and most distinguished liberal-arts colleges. All of them are private institutions, most are in the East. Despite the fact that my wife is a graduate of UCLA and I am a native Middle Westerner, I cannot claim intimate knowledge of the great public institutions of higher learning that dot the interstate highway map.

To counterbalance that obvious limitation, I offer one interesting set of professional experiences. In addition to my regular duties as faculty member and administrator, I have deliberately sought out the opportunity of working with institutional accreditation teams. All American colleges and universities are examined by regional accrediting agencies. These self-policing bodies, set up by the higher-education establishment, provide peer review of institutional worthiness. I have had the pleasure of serving on some dozen or more accrediting teams, in most instances as chairman. These institutions have ranged from Yale to the American University in Cairo, from the U.S. Naval Academy to Lyndon State in Vermont. They have included the most selective institutions and one charming college where I asked for the admissions policy and was told, "Sir, if they can hear thunder and see lightning we take 'em." Since the process of accreditation involves a lengthy written self-study and extensive on-campus interviews with students, faculty, and staff, plus the collective experience of the accreditation team of eight to ten individuals from other colleges, it is an experience that gives depth and range to one's views about what is happening in higher education.

Even accrediting experience on two continents would hardly qualify for discussing the range of universities and colleges on the American scene if it were not for the fact that, despite each and every college's claim to be *the* unique place for higher education, there is probably more homogeneity than diversity in the American academic world. In a certain sense, higher education constitutes a single national industry. The faculties are trained at a limited set of graduate institutions, and they move about relatively freely from coast to coast and up and down the putative prestige scale of academies. While I am sure that there are local differences in Portland, Oregon, that define a Reed student, there is a powerful uniformity of youth culture that assures the record producers and jeans makers that they can sell their products on any campus. One of the wisdoms of this book will be to note the commonality of the colleges rather than their claimed distinctiveness. Thus, despite the fact that neither myself nor the editor of the latest compendious guidebook can claim immediate knowledge of every root and branch of higher education, it is possible to survey the territory with some accuracy.

All that professional appointment in various universities may actually *dis*qualify an author. Everyone is deeply suspicious of the party line. Thus the rash of "insider" guides to colleges, for example *The Insider's Guide to Colleges*, which issues forth from the *Yale Daily News* every now and then. A curious reader might ask what qualifies one to be an insider when reporting on colleges and universities. One might even wonder whether the inside view is the *whole* truth even if it is nothing but the truth. An insider's view of the *QEII* might give only the boiler-room version of a Caribbean cruise. However, if "insider" suggests some intimate knowledge of collegiate reality not normally revealed by the PR office, then I would like to claim some title to being an insider. Faculty members and even university deans and presidents should have some inside knowledge about colleges. The boiler room certainly knows something, but then, so does the bridge.

3

Reason and Romance

I may have acquired curiosity about the "meaning of college" from watching Princeton sophomores fail out drop by drop, but a passion sufficient to write was aroused by a recent grand tour of colleges with a potential-freshman daughter. I was smitten with a strong desire to write something called *A Rational Parent's Guide to Colleges*. There are lots of problems with such a text and title. (Thus this book is not what I had planned, though it calmed the passions.) In the very first place, to what does "rational" apply? Parent, guide, or colleges? It is easy enough to wonder whether any of the above qualify for the designation. I am certain that parenting is not a scrupulously rational occupation either in its normal initiatory activities or in the long line of the parental career. Parents of college-bound high-school students may find rationality a particularly maladaptive life mode.

The rationality of any guide to colleges—including this book—will be shown in the course of the text. The rationality of colleges and universities will vary according to a reader's

Since it is the student who profits (or not) from higher education, the student is the ultimate insider: What happens (or doesn't happen) inside his or her head over four years will determine whether this college was a good one. True enough and not disputable. Nevertheless—sailing along with the metaphor of ships and cruises—the ability of the crew to explain the nature of the ship, the itinerary of the trip, and the valuable sights to see may be crucial to understanding the value of the voyage. I am not persuaded that our academic crew does a very good job in conveying the reality of colleges behind the tourist brochures of the admissions procedure.

I read recently that the plural of "anecdote" is "data." Experience of applying, studying, teaching, administering, and accrediting has given me a selection of anecdotal material (mostly true) which I have relied on to make sprightly the text of this treatment. Naturally I believe that my anecdotes epitomize data. Though I am scarcely a formal historian of higher education, I have had a special avocational interest in the histories of the institutions where I have served and in academic history overall. That is reflected in the text and is a balance to the personal tale. My philosophical interests are metaphysics and the philosophy of history, so finally this book is a "metaphysical history of education" so deeply disguised that no reader will be turned off by the very thought of it.

Metaphysical reflection (even in mask and veil) can be dank and dreary in my experience. That is the last thing I desire. Higher education is a lightsome place at best—full of wit and learning, sharp talk and wild ideas, the edge of science and the exuberance of the ever-young freshman class. It is worth the effort of application (pun intended). It is not my intention, however, to make the application burden heavier than it already is. The themes discussed in this small book are deep, broad, big, important, and similar adjectives of portent. I am under no illusion that they are explored as deeply, broadly, and portentously as they deserve. I have attempted to keep an appropriate distance, giving the reader a somewhat airy tour of academia. To write drearily about universities loses in spirit what it may gain in archival accuracy.

relative assessment of the value of classical Greek, radio astronomy, faculty meetings, fraternity parties, or alumni reunions. Finally, "rationality" may not be a wholly rational idea when it comes to understanding colleges.

The rationality I intended, however, rested on its root word *"ratio,"* the Latin for "reason." The English word "ratio" carries with it the mathematical meaning of "proportion." The ratio of a thing is its proportion to something else. In the case of universities the question is, "Proportional to what?" To most observers, colleges may seem just a fact of life. They may be no more "rational" than puberty, a necessity of nature that resists rational inquiry. But colleges and universities are curious cultural creations whose meaning can be "ratio"-ed against other ways and other worlds.

Colleges have not always been. The ancient world did not have them and most of the world's population today manages to get from generation to generation without taking SAT tests. Universities in any recognizable form are medieval in origin. It is not clear that American colleges retain anything but costumery from the days of Alcuin. It is not even clear that American colleges of the late twentieth century retain much from the late nineteenth century—or the 1930s. One needs to explicate the modern college by comparing and contrasting it with the *collegium* of yesteryear, in the usual format of a final exam.

One need not know the history of General Motors in order to visit Joe's Used Car Lot and this book is not an exercise in collegiate antiquarianism, but colleges are a different purchase. They are structured (and advertised) around a cluster of terms that, though they have certain *tone*, are scarcely definable by the average parent, student, taxpayer, or U.S. Senator. Should Junior study "liberal arts"? That sounds nice: Americans like to think "liberal" and "arts" suggests culture and refinement. But what is a liberal-arts education after all? There is an extraordinarily tangled history behind this hifalutin term. Some of that history actually determines what goes on in the classrooms at Old Main.

This essay is also not a compendium of catalogue copy and statistics. Guidebooks exist for that purpose and can be used profitably. My interest is rather different. As the prospective college consumer reads through the guides and brochures, as the newspaper reader scans the latest blast from the secretary of education, certain hot notions will surely emerge: liberal arts versus career, college versus university, teaching versus research, community of learning versus diversity of learners. Most of the time these terms are discussed in a decidedly vaporous manner. They are not used to describe historical realities but to suggest images which entice or appall.

For example, it would be extremely difficult to find a university or college anywhere that does not claim to offer students close personal attention. "At our institution [unlike Brand X University] teaching is taken seriously." I have never been able to locate Brand X University—at least, there are no institutioins that advertise that they have really smart faculty who don't fool around with laggard students: "Here at Braino State we expect students to shape up or ship out!"

In a recent survey undertaken at my own school we discovered that prospective applicants reacted negatively to the word "research." Even the very best high-school students, with the most impressive possibilities for undertaking advanced scholarship, shy away from the term. In contrast, "teaching" always has a positive connotation for students. This sharp contrast in the apprehension of the applicant has only the shadowiest relationship to academic realities. Faculty at major research universities can and do teach magnificently well, while faculty at our most distinguished teaching colleges always engage in scholarship and advanced research at or near the level of their university colleagues. Thus, to be sold on the notion of a Teaching College in contrast to Nonesuch Research Institute is mostly to purchase fiction for fact. That is not to say that there are not important differences between colleges, between colleges and universities, between liberal arts and professional programs, and so on, but they are seldom what the public myth and application advertising would suggest. My aim is to get Siwash without Hogwash.

Even more important than the strictly academic claims of universities are the large soul-enhancing opportunities suggested in the institutional prospectus. It isn't just an education one gets at Prestige U., it is "the Prestige *experience*." These are mighty claims of mighty importance to the prospective student and parent. They are also the most elusive. Jane Smith had a wonderful experience at P.U. but Joe Doe withdrew in disarray. In order to see how much and how far colleges can (or should) go in promising personality progress, I want to look closely at the current culture of colleges, professors, and youth in the dwindling days of the century. What can you rationally expect, in the psychic department, from the college of your choice? Four years in manual labor of the minor leagues will produce personality effects. What does Siwash offer in that line of goods?

One of the reasons that mere myth passes so easily as fundamental fact is that most people—including those within the halls of the academy itself—have so little historical sense of these peculiar institutions we call colleges and universities. In *The American College and University*, Frederick Rudolph noted that, at the time his book was written (1962), one could obtain a detailed monograph on almost any skirmish in the American Civil War, but *no* general history of American colleges existed. The field has improved slightly in the intervening years. But if there is now more scholarship about the historical character of these highly visible social institutions, there remain few readers. It will be a rare parent, applicant, or editorialist who will know anything at all about the history of the institutions being considererd or castigated. This book cannot hope to deal with the chronicles of 3,300-plus American institutions of higher learning, but it will suggest critical historical trends.

The plan of this small volume revolves around a series of connected discussions of some of the central issues of college-going. I want to explore the very most fundamental actors and plot line of any and all colleges and universities. A college or university is a place where people called professors teach something called the curriculum to people called students. Professors, students, and the curriculum are the deep mysteries to be revealed. I will argue that professors are a thoroughly modern invention not well understood; students (as youth) are even more modern and perhaps even less comprehensible. The curriculum? Also novel—and its deepest meaning is like to be misunderstood both by its masters and their charges.

Is college a mystery in broad daylight? Indeed. Consider again the rationality of college choice. The great Harvard sociologist, Talcott Parsons, has noted that individuals create pseudorational mythologies to justify inscrutable choices. College choice is one of the great inscrutables. Mythology abounds. In the year after Doug Flutie threw a last-second touchdown pass to beat Miami, admissions applications at Boston College shot up some 20 percent. At the time of his athletic heroism Flutie was a senior. None of those applicants could have hoped to see him play. Perhaps these young people chose B.C. because they liked winning football. Nothing wrong that—but a season ticket to the Patriots would be a lot cheaper and less strenuous than a Jesuit education.

Presumably no one—except a talented tackle—seeks higher education just for the athletics. (And if he is a *very* talented tackle, he will not be seeking but sought.) The eager applicants to B.C were fortunate in that they chose a strong academic school where they would get educational value in between bowl games. Nevertheless, it says something about the inscrutability of colleges that it may take national television and a "Hail, Mary" pass to create a decision procedure.

My belief in the Flutie factor is by no means based only on anecdotal evidence. In his sober study of American colleges and universities, former U.S. Education Commissioner Ernest Boyer concluded that the most important factor by far in the evaluation of colleges by parents and applicants was *the appearance of the campus*. When I was a dean of dropouts a common explanation from some unhappy withdrawer for his original decision to attend Princeton was, "I came here in the spring with my dad and the flowers really snowed me." Mixed metaphor aside, the horticultural principle of college choice is prevalent and powerful. When I was president at Bucknell, a generous donor offered us ten thousand tulip bulbs. I accepted them with eagerness. When the tulips bloomed, admissions applications rose.

Flowers and Flutie seem aptly labeled "romantic." What is interesting is that these aspects of the campus setting apparently have overwhelming influence in the choice of applicants and in setting the headlines of newspapers. Surely Doug Flutie is better known to the public than Don Monan. Monan has been the president of Boston College for nearly twenty years; personal interest would have me believe Don has meant more to B.C. than Doug has.

It may be difficult to discover a pure case of rational choice for college. One of the few that I know was told to me by Carlton Gadjusek, a 1976 Nobel Prize winner and a graduate of the University of Rochester. I asked why he had chosen Rochester. "Well," he said, "I was admitted at the age of sixteen to Harvard, Princeton, Rochester, and several other schools. I went to Harvard and went directly to the chairman of the physics department. I told him that there were three experiments I wished to carry forward on fundamental nuclear structures. The chair said, 'I am sorry, young man, but you have come to the wrong school. The only University with a functioning accelerator is Rochester.' So I packed my bags and transferred to Rochester."

I would regard Gadjusek's decision as a thoroughly rational university choice. Does one have to be a future Nobelist to make rational judgments? Relatively few college freshmen have a specific problem in nuclear physics to work out, and even Gadjusek made the wrong initial choice, which he subsequently had to correct.

To emphasize the crucial role of "romance" in college choice can of course be misleading. Romance is presumably not the whole story. Those flower-smitten freshmen of yesteryear who chose old Nassau had, without a doubt, already narrowed the field of choice to a selected list of very, very "rational" choices and were now looking for a mythology to gloss the facts. Yale's Gothic architecture, Dartmouth's snow, or California's sun might have won the day, but academic prowess was assumed.

Given a suppressed rationality in the process, should one really be concerned that romance wins the day? It usually does. Still the thoughtful applicant should avoid choosing a college on the basis of a "crush" just as much as he or she should avoid marrying on the basis of the more common variety. John Q. Public should have a better gauge of academic quality than the NCAA playoffs. If the rational basis for understanding is truly present, then let a thousand flowers bloom. But parents and the public can be misled by the lush ivy into regarding second-tier teaching as first-tier education.

Rationality is, as started earlier, a matter of proportion, ratioing x to y. Colleges need to be measured against modernity but they come in archaic disguise. The appearance that snows the hapless applicant is wildly anachronistic. If Jane Doe is dazzled by Yale Gothic, she really doesn't want medieval plumbing or the scholastic curriculum of rhetoric, logic, and dialectic. Behind those leaded windows there had better be a half-dozen electron microscopes. Spying high tech behind the buttresses is relatively easy, but what is not is detecting the *spirit of modernity* that defines all of contemporary higher education. The modern sense of colleges is strikingly different from the monastic or ministerial manners suggested by spires, flowers, fenestration, and the admissions brochure.

It is important to explain the persistent romance of American colleges. The American college is historically romantic and is likely to remain so. What happens to heartfelt higher ed in the modern (I call it scientific) mode? If the heart has its reasons, scientific reason has its own romance. The very best college experience requires passion; the principal danger in this quest is that one is looking for the wrong romance.

Though it seems irrational to praise colleges for the quality of their gardening, the fault lies deep in the history of American higher education. No matter how professionalized, scientific, or careerist American higher education may become, its deepest tug is not in practicality but in "going-to-college." Going-to-college is a stage on life's way. Because collegegoing is a rite of passage, like marriage and death, it is no surprise that applicants and their anxious parents look to college as much for life values as for science and learning. When I took my daughter on the grand admissions tour of some of our grandest colleges and universities, I was convinced that the major interest on each and every campus was swimming. Without fail, the new swimming pool was displayed with pride. It assured us, supposedly, that Ivy Sister College was interested in the whole (and clean) person.

The academic equivalent of the swimming pool is the "liberal-arts curriculum." Devotion or a nod to the liberal arts is necessary in every higher educational institution from Chico State on. Liberal arts is the essential romance of American collegiate education. For all that it singles out an ancient and honorable academic tradition, "liberal arts" is most frequently used in America in a special sense that is far from clear to anyone, including the catalogue writer.

There really are no liberal-arts colleges or universities outside the United States, with the interesting exception of a few American exports such as the American University in Cairo. This is not to imply that Oxford does not teach philosophy and French literature. Of course it does but the spirit is not Yankee liberal-artsy. To understand American liberal arts is to understand the romantic principles which underlie (or overlay) college in the United States.

American colleges stem ideologically from Protestant denominations. Colleges were consciously created in colonial times in America to provide a learned clergy when, as the founders of Harvard put it, "our current generation of ministers shall have been laid into dust." This origin is subtly different from that of our European counterparts. European universities, for all that they were creatures of the Catholic religious orders, did not see their mission as educating a clergy. Clergy were formed by the rules of the cloister, not the classroom. Students at the great medieval universities were as likely to be studying law—albeit canon law—as the Bible. Not so in America. Moral training (of Protestant clergy) gave energy to the initial phases of American education, and "moral" training has remained crucial to the present day. Puritanism in sex may have had its day, but protest readily replaces pulpit in the search for a heavenly city here and now, often on the college quad.

American colleges quickly abandoned an exclusive attention to clerical training, but the urge to spiritual formation remained. In the nineteenth century, the high point of the college year was the annual religious revival, an event every bit as important as the Penn State–Nebraska game. I recall a noteworthy entry in the Middlebury College chronicles: "1832: Great religious revival ends in disaster." It seems that in that year a group of overspiritualized young men ran naked in the streets of Middlebury and burned down several buildings. Today that happens after the Orange Bowl.

The liberal-arts curriculum and the liberal-arts collegiate institution are the most recent structural expression of this initial clerical urge. Scarcely a college or university in the country will not claim to be interested in more than the academic education of students. Although the current president of Princeton may, in his theology, be a far cry from President Jonathan Edwards, one can be certain that Harold Shapiro believes as deeply in the moral education of his students as the dour devine who preceded him in office.

The universal interest in liberal arts from Bowdoin to Berkeley is the root of American collegiate romanticism. American colleges have *always* stood for something more—and perhaps something more important—than mere academics. In earlier days that "something more" was easily identified with the creed and practice of some denomination. Denominational institutions still exist—Wheaton in Illinois, Calvin College in Michigan—but on the whole the older evangelical urge has diffused into football, fraternities, foreign study, friendship, fun, and flowers.

It is no surprise, then, that students and parents search for "something far more deeply interfused, / Whose dwelling is the light of setting suns" as the inner secret of American higher education. If they end up smitten with the campus flora and fauna, blame it on John Calvin.

Unfortunately for the sheer romanticism of college life, something else happened to the Presbyterian college of the past. Dilution is not the total tale. (Change also happened to the Jesuit university and other non-Protestant institutions, but for U.S. constitutional reasons as much as because of changing times or Pope John XXIII.) In the late nineteenth century, graduates of American colleges started to go to Europe for postgraduate training, since there was hardly anything worthy of the name in the United States. What they learned there was not only philosophy or medicine; they also acquired a different vision of higher education, not denominational in faith and practice, but professional and scholarly and "scientific." The twentieth century has been a complex and often muddled mix of moral motives for education (derived from the denominational past) and the scientific (European) urge of faculties. ("Scientific" is used with caution. It is the German *Wissenschaft*, which includes natural science but also a more critical research attitude toward all areas of study.)

It may be no mere accident that my example of a rational college choice was made by Carlton Gadjusek, who was a sixteen-year-old Czech refugee when he applied to Harvard, Princeton, Rochester, et al. It may be no accident that Vietnamese are victorious valedictorians across the land: The Vietnamese academic tradition is French. The Chinese and Japanese systems were German in spirit before the Americans moved into heavy hardware science and attracted so many students from the Pacific Rim. To vastly oversimplify, "Europeanized" faculty respond immediately to the "professional" ambitions of students emerging from a European tradition.

Students entering almost any contemporary college or university find themselves in a social institution that is still working out the complexity of a double tradition: American liberal-arts *moral* education and European scientific assumptions. Change and complexity in our institutions stem from the migration of future faculty from American liberal-arts institutions to European scholarly universities at the end of the nineteenth century.

If the changes that affect the full culture of the contemporary college were merely in the faculty, the story of this text would be far simpler. However, while faculty were being Europeanized, something even more noteworthy was happening to students. In the following chapters, I want to look at the modernization of the three simple components of any college. A college is a place where *students* learn from *faculty* via a *curriculum* of study. As indicated earlier, all three are veiled mysteries. I wish to lift the veil at least knee-high. I start with students.

4

Birth of Youth

To understand colleges requires archaeologic technique. Archaeology is a detective game we play with unknown and mysterious cultures of the past. By digging up pots and sifting rubbish heaps, we are able to piece together the character of vanished peoples who carelessly forgot to write down what they were up to.

It is odd that we need an archaeology for colleges and universities. Are they mysterious and unknown? There they are in all their psuedo-Gothic and mock-Georgian splendor. These historic companies of talkers and writers surely need no archaeologists. But they do. Various scholars of universities have noted that they are among history's most inarticulate communities—when speaking about *themselves*. University communities may have long advised the church or admonished the state, but they have been extraordinarily poor at keeping tabs on what was happening on campus. A researcher on student life in nineteenth-century Princeton was reduced to deducing results from library charge cards. At the beginning of the nineteenth century, Oxford University underwent two major reforms instigated by the government. These measures were to change radically the lazy Georgian institution of the eighteenth century into the significant scholarly institution of the next century and beyond. We know all the actors in the movement. We haven't a scrap of commentary by any of them on the rationale for the reform. The principal scholar of the reforms has been left to conjecture that it was probably some sort of reaction to the French Revolution!

The lack of written commentary on colleges and universities might not be any problem if the nature of these present-day imposing social institutions were well understood. The problem is that colleges are so new on the cultural scene that we are almost bound to misunderstand them. The Gothic fabric of the building suggests antiquity, but the architecture probably has as much relevance to the spirit of the enterprise as do the president's graduation robes, borrowed from some long-forgotten monastic costumer. If one looks seriously at the "old-time college of Grandfather's day (certainly Great-Grandfather's), present places appear as recent concoctions as air conditioning.

One could take the attitude toward colleges past that they belong to the world of quaintness, best left to curio seekers and academic archaeologists. There are two problems with that simple solution. In the first place we need *something* as a point of comparison for current colleges—to what shall they be proportioned? One might try banks or ashrams, but Old Siwash, for all its radical difference, is still a useful comparison point. More important, education suffers from a perpetual spiritual hangover. It never quite recovers from the spirit of last century's academic festivals. Max Beerbohm said of Oxford, "It is a place where nothing is ever born and nothing ever quite dies." One would have to change that saying in America (and at contemporary Oxford as well). In America a truly new education was born at the end of the nineteenth century, but we have not let the older one quite die—indeed, in our most sentimental moments, we even forget about the newborn as well.

One of the most interesting stories of collegiate continuity and radical change can be related by telling a tale of students. It is, after all, students who create colleges and universities. There have been learned societies and gatherings of savants for untold ages, but it is by adding students to be formally trained that a school is created. Because students constitute the essentials of a college, I sketch their story first.

Several years ago I was attending a planning session at Penn State University. The presenter was sketching out the challenges of the future and there was a fair amount of apprehension expressed by the audience about whether the radical changes necessary to meet any future would occur. Since Penn State had but recently celebrated the centennial of its founding, it occurred to me that anyone a century ago who had forecast the contemporary institution would have been regarded as a lunatic. Penn State was founded in 1855. If you had told the citizens of the Commonwealth in the 1850s that you intended to create a great "city of the young" with a population of 35,000 people between ages eighteen and twenty-two, this city to be governed by a small lot of physicists, philosophers, and musicologists, you would have been thought both imprudent and implausible. It was not possible that so many youth would be at schoool—they would mostly be married, with families, tilling the ancestral farm. And why would anyone want to break the family bonds at age eighteen and give over the nurturing of young people to such a collection of "schoolmasters"? ("Scholars" in the modern sense would have been virtually unintelligible in 1855.)

Such a simple comparison over only one century may jar the reader into a sense of the special—perhaps peculiar—nature of the American college. Most contemporary colleges and universities are dominantly age-segregated. When age segregation is combined with the common pattern of residential living, what else is created other than a "youth city"? In contemporary Egypt, college populations are dominantly youthful, but no self-respecting Egyptian would think of living outside the family until he or she is married. College students continue to function as part of the family and the general society throughout the college years in a manner quite alien to the contemporary American pattern. One should also not assume that the current pattern of residential facilities has been universal in American colleges. Martin Anderson, the first president of the University of Rochester, was steadfastly opposed to dormitories for students throughout the forty years of his tenure. His view was that students were much better off living with families; dormitories were devices of temptation. (More about that later on.)

The creation of such youth cities—social institutions unusual by most world cultural standards— has been paralleled (or caused by) a radical change in the meaning of going-to-college across the generations of American institutions. Ken Keniston, the psychologist, has given as brief, articulate, and, I believe, accurate account of the cultural change. To understand what it means for a contemporary son or daughter to "go to college" it is worth considering the cultural sense of the gesture. Going-to-college is a different journey to a different place than it was when Harvard College started it all in 1638.

In the earliest (colonial) period of collegegoing, young people went to college as "place holders." By and large the college population was composed of the sons (no daughters) of individuals who already had status in the society: ministers, lawyers, wealthy men of affairs. The young person saw college as a way of continuing the family position in society. This cultural assumption remained dominant until about the time of the American Civil War. After the war we see the emergence of the "Horatio Alger" scenario. Now, there were "place getters," men who went to college to advance in American society. They sought positions socially and economically "better" than their fathers'. (Women began to attend colleges at this time, but not for social advance. Since college women did not normally enter the world of work, the curriculum and social expectations of the college aimed to produce women who would offer moral refinement and balance to the commercially oriented spouse.)

My father was a place getter who attended a place-getting institution, a type of college which had a special vogue in the late nineteenth century. Clark University was founded by Jonas Clark as a "poor boy's" college. Through generous endowment, Clark, a successful Worcester merchant, furthered the American aspiration for generational advancement. My father, the son of an Irish immigrant farm laborer, was urged by his mother to do better. Since he became a successful physician, Clark's hopes were realized.

Keniston sees in the 1920s the most significant shift in the meaning of going-to-college, and he associates the new meaning with the rise of intercollegiate athletics. Big- and little-time athletics is so much part of the contemporary collegiate scene that it may be difficult to realize that colleges in America have lived without sports for most of their historical existence and that the rest of the world's universities somehow manage to educate youth with no more sports program than a cinder track.

What is the importance of big-time intercollegiate athletics, a creation largely of the post–World War I collegiate culture? For Keniston, it is the emergence for the first time (perhaps in world history) of the notion that youth is a time of attainment. Prior to big-publicity college sports, it is hard to imagine that a twenty-year-old could become a national cultural hero. A halfback can do something in youth that constitutes a peak attainment. (In order to keep commonality of nomenclature, I call this the place-kicking phase of American collegiate culture.) In the two earlier phases college is a stage *on the way* to adulthood, career, and social position. In the "place-kicking" phase, for the first time one has the sense that it is not necessary to define college by what comes after. College is not necessarily on the way to an "adult" life but is itself a way of life.

The emergence of a separate college culture is clearly marked in images of the period. My father recalled his great pleasure (as a place getter) in the shift from knickers to long trousers that marked the sartorial change to college. Long pants were a sign of adulthood, and at college one took on the manners of adulthood. In the twenties a distinctive *collegiate* costume emerged with the raccoon coat and the other appurtenances of jazz-age youth.

Not only dress but collegiate social institutions began a slow cultural change. Fraternities were largely the creation of the place-getting phase of university culture. They were a reaction to the dominant academic culture, which smacked too much of the minister's manse for the ambitious place-seekers of the day. The fraternity was the linkage to the adult world of business manners and commercial conversation. It is interesting to read the minutes of nineteenth-century fraternity affairs. "Brother Smith returned from Philadelphia and discussed his position as head cashier at First Pennsylvania." The linkage between undergraduates and adult alumni was extremely strong, befitting the role of the fraternity in getting members places in the adult world after college. In the twenties, fraternities became much more instruments of an independent youth culture than a training ground for the Union League Club. This trend has continued apace to the present day.

The final phase of this cultural progress of colleges emerged after World War II and was marked, in Keniston's judgment, by the emergence of a full-blown youth culture in America. Youth is not only a time of attainment, it is itself an attainment. The effect of youth culture on prominent youth institutions like colleges and universities is extraordinary. If previous phases were place holding and place getting, the new phase (at its worst, I suppose) is labeled by Keniston place outing. College is not only its own culture, it becomes the only culture. College is not a way toward adulthood or anything else—college is arrival. This trend was certainly most noticeable in the sixties and seventies, when many universities were surrounded physically by large communities of continuing graduate students, dropouts, and last year's valedictorian bartending because he or she couldn't bear to leave the confines of collegiate culture. In the sixties I used to give a talk entitled "Is There Life After College?" because it seemed to me that so many of our students had such a wonderful experience at Middlebury that they

couldn't face the cruel world postcollege. And I couldn't believe that even Vermont could absorb that number of candle-
stick makers and tie-dye artists.

If a football serves as an emblem of the twenties youth
culture, the transistor will do for the contemporary scene. In
the 1930s radios were cumbersome, expensive affairs full of
glass tubes. The family would buy a Stromberg-Carlson con-
sole and place it square in the living room as *the* family radio
box. The transistor miniaturized the sets and made portable
noise extraordinarily inexpensive. No longer was *the* radio
pouring out Fibber McGee and similar family entertainment;
now a second radio belonged to the young of the family, and
they could have music other than Fred Waring.

The music that flowed down from the magnetic heavens
into the transistor was not only other than adult music, it often
seemed counter-adult music. In the 1930s the family could sit
by the big mahogany cabinet to hear the Bob Hope show with
his perennial theme song: "Thanks for the memory / Of your
lips next to mine / The Parthenon, castles on the Rhine / And
moonlight on the Hudson River Line. . . ." The Parthenon—
even from Bob Hope—was a worthy cultural aspiration befitting a sophisticated adult goal. What do you do with "You
ain't nothin' but a hound dog"? Anxious parents and school-
teachers might come to believe the message of Pink Floyd's
hit single of 1983: "We don't need no education." "Education"
comes from the Latin *educere* (to lead: *ducere*; out of: *ex*). If
youth is arrival, "We don't need no leading out of."

One might regard rock and roll and its ideological accom-
paniments as just another one of those means by which the
younger generation scandalizes the older. The waltz was once
regarded as a vile dance. Although I will discuss these matters
at length later in the book, it is important to note that some
sort of change was going on in the colleges alongside of and
perhaps with the accompaniment of the new music. Colleges
in the postwar years simply dropped the theory of acting in
loco parentis. Dormitories were opened, drinking regulations
were relaxed, and drug problems were winked at or relegated

to the local police department. Acting "in the place of the parent" was a concept which would have pleased colonial place-holders who wanted to hold the place of the parent. The concept didn't take in the 1960s.

The final snapshot of colleges circa the 1990s might picture a rampant, independent youth culture flourishing in every academic grove. But recent observers of the student species have suggested that we have returned to place holding and place getting. Students are supposedly obsessed with jobs, and the "practical" curricula are overflowing. It is the age not of the hippie but of the yuppie.

Two comments: Cultural distinctions across collegiate history are never clear-cut. In each age there have been place holders and even in colonial times there were dropouts and careerists. It is the new type that attracts interest. The notoriety of novelty may make us believe the society is simpler than it actually is.

My second observation is that whatever the careerist ambitions of the contemporary student, some permanent seismic change that marks a new era occurred in the 1960s in the culture of the young and their colleges. At the risk of revealing my metaphysical hand, I would characterize the difference as a change from *being* to *doing*. When my father contemplated college he wanted to *be* a doctor. To be a doctor was to fulfill a set of moral, social, and economic expectations that gave one a sense of self. Today the problem is more likely to be What shall I *do?* than What shall I *be?* One may choose to do medicine or law or engineering, but these professions do not dictate a life-style as in the past.

What changed in the sixties was life-style—witness the various sexual revolutions, which seem now to be fully accepted. It can be argued that the life-style remains some variation on youth style. Life is not my father trading knickers for long pants, it is blue jeans right on through. Can one make youth a life-style, yea unto middle age? Consult the quintessential sixties youth magazine, *Rolling Stone*, which has followed its readers right on through to gray hair. In Great Britain no one past the age of eighteen reads rock and roll magazines; in the United States the rock magazines have aged with the customer. My favorite recent example of the aging of *Rolling Stone* was a multipage picture spread of balding rock stars with their children. There may be hope yet for adulthood.

My sense of the contemporary student/college scene convinces me that we are not going back to the "silent generation" of 1950s careerists (my generation). How could one characterize the contemporary college student as "gray flannel"? The deepest past of American colleges settled the question "What should I be?"; the answer was, "A Christian gentleperson," perhaps. The old-time college incidentally helped in what one might do: practice medicine. The modern college is excellent (better) at what students should do. It is what they should be that remains a puzzle. If the colleges aren't entirely sure on that issue, someone—maybe Bruce Springsteen—will be of assistance.

This "archaeological" construction of the college has concentrated on artifacts of youth culture: library cards, fraternity notes, footballs, and rock music. I lead with it because college is a social institution of and for youth. As "youth" is understood in the culture, so the college will be subtly altered and defined. Fifteenth-century paintings of babies (as in scenes of Christ and the Virgin) often seem odd to us. They don't look like babies at all; they look like wizened adults. And so they were—because the view of childhood was that it was proto-adulthood. Children were distinctly unfinished. So with colleges. When students were seen (and saw themselves) as unfinished adults, then the college in loco parentis could take on the job of finishing them up to be adults: economically, socially, philosophically, ontologically, and any other way one might devise. If the assumption that students are unfinished changes, the sense of the collegiate culture changes.

I have my doubts that President Timothy Dwight's Yale was "fun"—he would have abhorred the idea. But, to the extent that both tutor and student regarded college years as on-the-way-to-fulfillment (adulthood, career, Christian commitment), there was no split between the stated activity of the establishment and the deepest sense of the clientele. Everybody believed in life after college, whatever their different versions of that "adult" heaven might be. What happens to college-as-youth-institution when the sense of "youth" changes? That is a difficult enough question, but it is made even more complex by the change in faculty that occurred at the same time as the change in youth. The next chapter traces the change in faculties. One (pessimistic) reading might be that new-minted youth and newfangled faculty meet under the aegis of outworn collegiate myth. No wonder college doesn't seem to be fun.

5

The Invention
of Professors

While youth was in the process of being born, professors were being invented. The meeting of newborn youth and the newly discovered professor is the conjunction that Americans call going to college.

Having sketched out the birth of youth, the obvious next step is to describe the character of faculties to see how profs and sophs mix and match. Given the character of the thoroughly modern professor, is he or she academic adviser or adversary? Experts disagree in their assessment. Clark Kerr, a former president of the California university system and distinguished former labor mediator, saw faculty and students as natural antagonists. The students want maximum teaching attention; the faculty, free time for research. It is the role of the administrator to mediate this characteristic conflict. Philosopher Paul Goodman, on the other hand, saw faculty and students as natural friends. Their happy communion was marred by the presence of busybody bureaucrats like President Clark Kerr. Which side is correct about the modern professorate?

"Professors" have not been around much longer than youth. As a professor of philosophy, I am acutely conscious of this. Most of the celebrated philosophers of the past were anything but professors. Spinoza was a lens grinder, John Locke secretary to the Lord High Chancellor, Leibniz was—if anything—a librarian. There were clerics who were professors, like Thomas Aquinas, but they were monks first and professors as an after-thought. It isn't until Immanuel Kant that one can find something like a professor of philosophy in the modern sense. (Kant was famous for his lectures on geography.)

At least there have been philosophers since ancient days with or without academic tenure; one may be even more tenuous if one is, say, a "psychologist." One of my predecessors as president of Bucknell University (also of Rochester), David Jayne Hill, was the first person ever in the history of academia or anything to style himself a psychologist, as Hill did in 1883. (If one were to read Dr. Hill today on "psychology," one would find that his work bears only a distant relation to the modern discipline.) The current staff of colleges and universities was not created by putting "professor of" before the name of some ancient study like philosophy; most contemporary studies were invented but recently, along with the professors who profess them.

A case in point from family history: My grandfather Fehlandt took appointment at Ripon College in 1914. Grandfather was a well-educated fellow, having studied at the University of Wisconsin, Yale Divinity School, and Princeton Theological Seminary. Grandfather accepted an appointment in "sociology." To the best of my knowledge, Grandfather didn't know a thing about "sociology"—in fact, the study had been "invented" well after he left formal schooling.

(To give Grandfather a break, one has to consider the history of the development of sociology as an academic study. The roots of the discipline lie partly in the YMCA movement of the late nineteenth century. The social concerns of the YMCA led individuals associated with the organization to investigate the nature of social problems. It was impossible to believe that the plight of the clients they served was wholly due to individual failure; there was something about the structure of the social organizations surrounding the poor and delinquent that had to be understood and changed. Sociology was the formal con-glomeration of these informal studies, and one might date its origin from the foundation of the American Sociological Association in 1906. Grandfather was not and could not have trained as a sociologist since the subject matter was scarcely invented by the time he claimed to profess it, but he was deeply involved in the YMCA effort and so aware of the proto-literature of the field.)

Similar tangled tales can be told about the recent emergence of almost all modern subject matters out of the industrial laboratory, the gentleman's study, or the floor of the bourse. History itself was scarcely recognized as a discipline in any of the world's universities until the end of the eighteenth century. Departments of English are scarcely a century old. In the 1850s, Charles Eliot (president of Harvard from 1869 to 1909) was the first student ever at Harvard to do a laboratory science. (And he was able to do so because his professor had outfitted a laboratory in his private residence.) I mention here only "traditional" curricula like Chemistry. (The American Chemical Society was founded in 1883.) It is obvious enough that much of what fills the catalogues of contemporary colleges is novelty incarnate: computer science, communication arts, cost accounting (a profession virtually unknown in America until the 1920s).

The explanation of the invention of professors can only be undertaken when we discuss the nature of the modern idea of higher education, which emerged at the beginning of the twentieth century. Simply stated, the "classical curriculum," with all its tedious exercises and deeper rationalities was replaced by the "scientific curriculum" and its attendant masters, the modern professors of X and Y and Z. Because the shift from classical to scientific is so important—and continues to be a debatable issue, as in Allan Bloom's diatribe against the modern university, *The Closing of the American Mind*—I will discuss the curriculum in due course. For now, however, I want to point out some career characteristics that differentiate "the professor" from Grandfather Fehlandt.

In the previous chapter we discussed some qualities of "youth" that create tension between the social setting of college (as a youth institution) and education's apparent inner rationale (a scheme for "leading out" into something: maturity, career, citizenship). If there is an interesting inner tension between Youth and Old U., there is another and different inner tension between professors and the institutions of education. Grandfather continues to be a case in point.

Grandfather left a pastorate in North Dakota to assume his duties at Ripon, but to him this did not seem like a full-scale change in career. If you read histories of the period you will find that faculty were not "appointed"; they were "called" to their collegiate positions. College teaching was a "vocation," not a job or career. Grandfather had been called to the pulpit in Lakota, and now he was called to sociology at Ripon. The distinction between a calling and an appointment is not merely linguistic.

In one sense, of course, the collegiate "calling" reflected the denominational color of the older colleges. (Ripon was staunchly Congregationalist.) The romantic-religious heritage of American colleges emphasized spiritual enlightenment beyond mere academic instruction. It is obvious enough that, as the religious overlay of our colleges disappeared, the older religious sense of "calling" withered. As the sense of calling diminishes it is replaced by individual *expertise* (Grandfather had it not). The root cause of this change is the "scientific" assumption of the modern university.

Whatever the exact cause of the change from calling to appointment, the effect has been to diminish the bond between faculty and institution. Modern faculty are experts; they possess a skill that is their own, which they have labored lo! through a Ph.D. and beyond to "own." The old pastor/professor was "called" because the enlightenment of the Holy Spirit was not exactly something that one could own even with a degree from

Princeton Theological. The expert is an individualist in the sense that he or she can move from place to place and retain the owned skill. The pastor needs a place that calls for preaching. Thus, the old-style professor had an attachment to place that the modern expert need not feel. The modern attachment is to the field. One is a physicist first, and then one is a professor at Dartmouth or Ripon or Coe.

It is important to note the nature of the old pastoral attachment because, there are, of course, extraordinarily important attachments that modern faculty may have to particular institutions. If you want an accelerator in your backyard you will certainly want to be at Berkeley. (Rochester is out of accelerators but has the National Laboratory for Laser Energetics.) Mathematicians dote on Princeton because it is the only place where it is even statistically possible to meet someone in the supermarket who knows about your topological specialty. Faculty have their own prestige scales, and naturally they would like to be at one of the premier places for their respective fields. But the modern attachment to place only emphasizes the sense in which field of specialization has replaced spiritual calling. It is the best chemistry or the most advanced linguistics that attracts. The institution is the place where the tools of the field happen to be.

While the development of experts as faculty detaches them from institutional place, at the same time it has had the paradoxical effect of increasing the authority of faculty within their institutional settings. There have been several studies of "the old-time college president." To the new-time college president, like myself, he often appears as a figure to be envied. College presidents (old style) were plenipotentiary—they made virtually all the decisions. Charles Eliot reformed Harvard almost singlehandedly. (Not, of course, without opposition, which reached such a pitch that he was actually fired by the Board of Overseers whilst enjoying a summer trip to Europe. Happily, the board couldn't get its act together to appoint a successor, so Eliot simply returned in the fall, reoccupied his office, and continued for some twenty years in a highly successful tenure of office. There is much to be said for the ways of our ancestors.)

At regular intervals there appears an article in some earnest Sunday supplement: "What Happened to the Great University Presidents of Yesteryear?" The article will cite Eliot, Princeton's McCosh, Johns Hopkins's Daniel Coit Gilman, and so on—a parade of powerful nineteenth-century educational pioneers. These "captains of erudition" (Veblen's phrase) were the counterparts of the great business entrepreneurs of their day. Some, like John D. Rockefeller, teamed with like-spirited educators (William Rainey Harper) and founded great institutions (the University of Chicago). What happened to the great (old-style) presidents is what happened to pastoral professors: They were replaced by modern faculty.

Under the pastoral assumptions of the old-style college, the president was "chief minister" unto the congregation called. He was to be the assurance of orthodoxy. Professors served under the assumptions of a denominational regime of which the president was the chief curator. (In the earliest incorporation of the Baptist University at Lewisburg—later Bucknell—the board members were called curators. The presidents were surely keepers of the faith!) When faculty are no longer keepers of the denomination but experts in a discipline, they possess an authority over and above (sometimes over and against) the institution and its traditional faiths. If there were to be new-style faculty there had to be a recognition of their new authority. So much for authoritarian presidents.

If one looks closely at the great presidents of yesteryear one finds that it is not proper to class them with the pastoral dictators of the more distant past. Their story is more complex and illustrates the change in professorial status. The presidents mentioned above were great *reformer* presidents, and they were reforming the old denominational-classical college into the modern research university. Gilman and Harper were creating *new* universities whose main thrust was to be advanced scholarship and research; Eliot was reforming a significant college (Harvard) while McCosh took a rather insignificant backwater institution (Princeton) and converted it to modern greatness.

The authority of these great presidents was a powerful mix of the habits of old-style denominationalism and the new authority of the academic disciplines. Paradoxically, the presidents' success guaranteed that they would not have successors in kind. It was the disciplines and their faculties that were established in the new universities. Faculties became the establishment and the authority of the old-style president waned apace.

A sign of the new-style professorate is the topsy-turvy state of faculty unions. Unions are established to give authority and power to their members against owners and managers. It seems clear enough from the history of the older presidential dictatorships that establishing faculty authority is important and inevitable. Unionization seems a plausible vehicle. Unfortunately, by the time unionization became accepted by faculties, they had already gone past the point of unions—or at least that was the opinion of the U.S. Supreme Court. In *N.L.R.B. vs. Yeshiva University*, the court ruled that faculty couldn't unionize because they were not workers but managers. There may be fundamentally economic or sheerly political reasons for faculty unions, but in the ideology of universities it is clear that faculties are the authorities and managers. Realizing the importance of faculty authority is essential in developing an understanding of the modern sense of going-to-college.

A sign of new times was the emergence of the American Association of University Professors (AAUP), which was established in 1916. We hear so much these days about "academic freedom" and "tenure"; it is instructive to note that these phenomena have only barely emerged as of the founding of the AAUP. Academic freedom and tenure are rationally connected to the new discipline-oriented scientific meaning of the university. If disciplines transcend denominations, then they have a separate authority and consequent freedom, which cannot be abrogated by older assumptions. (Tenure comes after a probationary period during which the new teacher proves his or her authority in the field. Demonstrated authority leads to freedom to profess.) There was a string of cases following the turn of the century in which new-style faculty had brushed against old-style religious, patriotic, or political assumptions. Dismissals had ensued, and the new professorate needed to assert the freedom of their discipline from such machinations.

The tension of the transitional period from denomination to discipline can be seen in the debates of the initial meeting of the AAUP. The freedom asserted by faculty was a freedom of research in their scholarly discipline. What was *not* asserted was the freedom of faculty to teach whatever they wanted in any setting of their choosing. The original documents of the AAUP make a distinction between freedom of research, which needs to be protected, and the right of colleges to control (by some means) curriculum for the too young and impressionable. Originally AAUP was as stated: an association of *university* professors. Only university professors, because they were researchers, could be guaranteed freedom. *College teachers*, in contrast, had the responsibility of passing on the accumulated truths, wisdoms, cultures, or dogmas of the day; they were specifically excluded from the original scope of academic freedom.

The delicacy of the original AAUP discussion has long since gone. "Research freedom" has been extended to "teaching freedom" on almost every campus in the land. Although academic freedom in the broadest sense appears to be academic apple pie, the issues delineated originally by the AAUP remain controversial. Whenever there is a debate about curriculum somewhere, the argument about a "core" of knowledge which must be (morally? intellectually?) conveyed will emerge. If Professor Bloom is to be believed, students going off to college are in danger of imminent moral destruction because thoroughly modern faculties have given over transmitting a heritage in a riot of research.

For the moment, I will leave the state of the modern university or college as the simple(?) conjunction of modern students and modern faculty, a meeting place for Youth and Scientists. Place-holding or place-getting youth who (may) have let go of (some or all of) the spiritual assumptions of Pop and Mom (surely of grandparents) are educated, trained, or resisted by independent-minded, discipline-oriented, managerial, authoritative scholars. How does this encounter work at all?

6

"Give Me That Old-Time Religion!"

I f the modern college and the experts who staff it are of such relatively recent date in the great march of civilization, what have people been doing all these years since Bologna opened its doors in the eleventh century or colonial William and Mary in 1693? The history of higher ed has been a story of commercial and classical interests, curiously combined. (Only recently—in the last seventy years—have we had "science.")

A historical example illustrates the commercial aspect's *ab initio*. The University of Montpelier, in France, was founded in 1289 as a by-product of the spice business. Spice merchants trading out of the port of Montpelier on the Mediterranean took to selling the "lore of spices" in the off-season. In 1289 the lore was not culinary but medicinal, and so the first university school of medicine was created. It may be symbolic that the harbor has long since silted up but education has persevered.

Much of the impetus for the earliest universities was what

we might regard as professional studies. Professional theology enjoyed a readier market in thirteenth-century Paris than it does today, but even in those days most students attended universities to be trained as bureaucrats or (canon) lawyers for the church and court. As a means to the study of medicine or theology or canon law, the works that a twentieth-century university would relegate to the category of classics were given continuing attention. One needed Latin to function, since it remained the common learned language up to the very recent past. In the late eighteenth century, Kant wrote some of his works in Latin, and—though his major works were in German—in argument he preferred that his questioner pose the issue in Latin since he found it much clearer. (At the end of the nineteenth century, a French group of neo-Kantians caused *Die Kritik der reinen Vernunft* to be translated into Latin— presumably because the French have never been favorable to learning German. Kant would have been pleased.)

The study of Latin, Greek, and the masters thereof is not in itself the making of a curriculum. To create the "classical curriculum" of traditional denominational colleges one needed a basic assumption about the nature of education. The theory of education that lay behind the so-called classical curriculum of the old-style eighteenth- and nineteenth- century colleges will be variously praised or condemned according to one's reading of human nature. To its proponents, then and now, a classical curriculum suggests a deep commonality of humankind over the ages and through the regions of our habitation. One can grasp the meaning of the classical curriculum by seeing what opposed it and what finally destroyed it: the spirit of natural science. Those who established the classical curriculum believed that the deepest and most valuable truths to be known had already been discovered. How alienating from the heroic past, from civilizations ruined and gone, it would be to think that these great states and noble cultures did not share at the most fundamental level a sense of the essentials of human life. The impetus of natural science calls that assumption into question. The truth is *not* already available.

Aristotle thought the earth was the center of the universe! Truth is not at hand in the monuments of the past; it is to be discovered in the future, through investigation.

Although medieval universities may have been by-products of trade and theology, the lore to be sold to pupils was already available. Medicine was not the outcome of research, but a compilation of the wisdom of the ancients, such as Galen. This classical assumption (roughly speaking) dominated the universitites of the Old and New Worlds up to the end of the nineteenth century. In that classical world, there were "professors" and "students," but the assumptions behind their study was so radically different from those of the present day that it is not an exaggeration to claim that the professors one is likely to meet on the contemporary quad are as modern as the computers they program.

Professors (old style) who lived in the world of the classical curriculum would see no point to "research." Truth being already revealed and writ down, the principal arts were those of reading, writing, and interpretation. Grammar, elocution, and elegant exercises in high-style Latinity (or its modern-language descendant) were the tasks of the day. The old-style professor can be (perhaps unkindly) characterized as a drill master whose principal pedagogical gifts were persistence and punctiliousness.

When John Henry Cardinal Newman wrote his famous *Idea of a University* in 1852 as a prospectus for the new university in Dublin that he had been asked to head, his argument revealed the tension of the older classical assumptions. Although *Idea* is a favorite text for college commencement addresses in search of eloquent quotations, the institution Newman envisaged was about to pass from history. Newman's theory of the university was fundamentally classical. The basic truths were already known—a notion only reinforced, of course, by the assumptions of a revealed religion. Newman was aware of different currents. He recognized that there was this other world of research—but, in the clearest indication of the tension of his educational world, research was to be carried on outside the universities, in specialized institutes. The basic mission of the university was to pass on the common, fundamental, known wisdoms of the race. Newman's *Idea* was the last great configuration of the classical university; that Idea has been almost wholly superseded by the *scientific* university. In the scientific university the faculty cannot play drill master because the drill is not known.

The older classical curriculum which depended on eternal wisdoms, the *philosophia perennis*, has come to be deeply doubted in the present age. Science seems to have refuted so many obvious, eternal, certain truths that any curriculum that stands on dogma—classical or ecclesiastic—will be held in deep suspicion. If Christ or Cicero were heroes of a past ped- agogy of asserted truth, Socrates is often regarded as the hero of the modern curriculum, despite the fact that he "did his thing" in the now late, abandoned classical curriculum. A modern professor will readily claim title to the Socratic method. As practiced by the original, the method consisted of asking questions, not giving answers, because Socrates claimed to know nothing. He hoped that by needling his interlocutors he could pick up some shards of wisdom. If there is no "drill for truth," then something like the Socratic style of "professing" seems wholly appropriate.

There was a legendary figure—I assume (and hope) he was legendary—at Princeton, who had been assigned to teach in a course called Humanities 101–102. This was a throwback to the classical curriculum, since it covered world (largely Western) civilization from Adam to existentialism. The hero of my legend appears to have been thoroughly modern and thoroughly "Socratic." He rejected the whole notion of a march through "classical" texts. He announced at the begin- ning of his discussion sessions that he had never read any of the books in the course and that he never intended to: Why should he, since truth lay ahead, not in the past. The job of the students was to convince him each week that the book assigned was really worth reading.

I mention this legendary epitome of Socratism in order to

illustrate a fundamental problem of the contemporary college. Although a quarrel over ancient and modern curricula may seem to the average applicant something "merely academic," best left to windy faculty meetings, no less a person than the former secretary of education, William Bennett, has accused colleges of selling their civilizing classical birthright for a mess of trendy pamphlets. Bennett and Bloom, among others, see a "treason of the clerks" as faculties, in rejecting the surety of the classics, have given over the curriculum to the merest political fashions. If one really knows nothing, any drift of thought from the marketplace will do, won't it?

Perhaps it would be well to take the lesson of Socrates seriously. Socrates is (as usual) a paradoxical figure—he was, after all, condemned to death for corrupting youth. Socrates as a modern academic hero should be highly problematic. Universities and their professors would hardly be willing to accept the whole load of Socratic assumptions. Socrates said that he didn't know anything, and he was consistent enough not to take any money for his "teaching": I have nothing to give; why should you pay me for it? Few modern professors are *that* Socratic. Nor should universities be very happy with pure Socraticism. Because knowledge was so scarce, Socrates went searching for it everywhere in the society. It was Socrates' disillusioned pupil, Plato, who founded the *academy*—a place apart where one undertook specialized investigations toward truth. Socrates philosophized in the marketplace. He can hardly be the patron saint of specialized places of learning or of the faculty wage scale.

Bloom and Bennett sniff nihilism in the modern curriculum. Don't Socrates and science say that they know nothing? If so, what is the difference between such a declaration and despair, nihilism, angst, and the other tropes of modern advanced fiction? If college *Waiting for Godot* on the quad?

Embarrassing as it may be, one has to admit that professors do know *something* and that universities and colleges are particularly important places to go to learn it. But what? The charm of the classical curriculum was that it could point to the Truth—in the Bible, in Homer, and in the assembled masters of the ancient world. The modern university may seem to be only a promisory note on an extraordinarily distant (but verified) future. Will Mr. Godot *ever* turn up?

To summarize a complex situation: Modern faculties teach method, not matter. Science is not a completed compendium of "truths," but "the scientific method" is "universally" accepted as the only way toward the truth. Allegiance to "method" as the "subject matter" known and taught (at a tuition fee) is the crux of the modern university. This is true not only of the obvious "sciences" but of the former outposts of the classical curriculum. Literature, history, philosophy—even the "classics"—emphasize a way of thought as the object of study.

The distinction between method and matter is good as far as it goes, but doesn't quite make it to the goal line. More can be said in a "dogmatic" way about the scientific curriculum than at first appears. In its desire to distance itself from denominationalism, the contemporary university overstates its case. It is not uncommon to have a leading physicist on some state occasion—say, when he or she is receiving the Nobel Prize—proclaim a modesty about what is known that passes into utter skepticism. While these statements pay tribute to the Nobelist's moral character, they don't contribute much to the understanding of science or its modern creature, the university.

The fault in a curriculum of sheer method is that no one should be inclined to toil away on a method unless there are some demonstrated results. The reason the method of science is so valuable is that we really do know, in some more-or-less realm of absolute surety, certain truths. The earth really *is* more or less round. In a non-boastful manner, one ought to speak about the achievements of modern science. Physics, rather than fumbling nihilistically in the dark, is one of the greatest accomplishments of human imagination and community. Ditto for most of what goes on in the contemporary university—and one should include the classics along with chemistry. In many ways we read Homer "better" now because

of "scientific classical research" than did the drill masters of
the revered texts of yesteryear. We have learned more from
the texts by questioning them than by revering them.

Not only can modern methods produce true matter, no
method is without some fundamental truths about the method.
If we hold that there is a proper method of learning the truth,
then it is because we have already made certain assumptions
about the nature of how things stack up. The older classical
curriculum believed in the method of authorities. Given the
general darkness of the human condition, one should pay special heed to the few great souls who seem to have transcended
the human condition with immortal words and deeds. Socrates'
provisional skepticism rested on his experience of inability in
the supposed wise of the day. He came to believe that only
the gods were wise, but also that truth was somehow already
buried in the unconscious. Because truth was always pressing
in on our consciousness from forgotten Forms, his investigations were not nihilistic niggling at his nitwit contemporaries—
as they thought—but earnest searches for immortal memories.

It is important to emphasize where the classical and scientific
curricula agree. The virtue of the classical approach was that
it believed in truth. How many colleges have as their motto
"Ye shall know the truth and the truth shall make you free"?
From the standpoint of a defender of the classics like Bloom,
the modern university is nihilistic; it believes in nothing; there
is no truth, only a relativity of opinion; one culture is as good
as the next; and Popeye is as good as Plato. (Better, perhaps,
because Popeye is a populist.) For defenders of the scientific
spirit, Bloom is a dogmatist who arrogantly has designated *his*
(very definitely *his*) tradition as the truth. In the spirit of open
investigation that marks the modern scientific university we
must bring other voices to the table.

This current quarrel is important because it reveals the
strengths and weaknesses of the two traditions. The weakness
of the older classicism was certainly its complacency and
closedmindedness. Yet Bloom has a point that there can be
an equal closedmindedness and new complacency in a thoroughly modern curriculum. If the assumption of the scientific

curriculum is that all opinions are to be heard because we have no idea which is correct and any opinion will do, the mind might as well close down. Deciding on spinach is a matter not of mind but of taste. (Except for Popeye, of course.) If higher education is only a menu from all the world's cuisines, it may be delightful and intriguing but it will not call for intelligent judgment of truth.

There is no real reason to suppose that the essential nature of the scientific university is nihilistic, as Bloom would have us believe, but it may seem so. If the essential character of the modern university is, after all, scientific, that is because it demands verification and is prepared to place under rigorous examination any received opinion, from the fact that the sun rises in the east and sets in the west (false) to the inevitable rise of the proletariat (?). The whole point of investigation is verification, i.e., ascertainment of the truth. The classics are "opened up" as a means of investigation toward the truth. The classical curriculum had no trouble bearing allegiance to *the* truth—because its adherents believed truth was already at hand, thanks to the Greeks and Jews.

Freshmen students arriving in any September on any quad across the country are most likely to find the curriculum in continuing crisis. That is by no means a bad thing provided that the curricular quarrels rest on principle, not short-sighted politics. The issue between the classical and the scientific curriculum remains unsettled. Each side tends to view the other polemically. The need to reject past dogma, embedded in the classics of yore, leads moderns to boast too loudly of their skepticisms. This in turn leads traditionalists to spy nihilism under every negative. Dogmatically, I would assert that the older classical curriculum was too dogmatic, too narrowly confined, too concerned with literary elites, and biased in favor of certain classes and one gender. The open curriculum of science is preferable and the best we have. Nevertheless, it cannot rest on rejection. Man and woman do not live by refutation alone. The contemporary curriculum does not need a new dogmatism but a new dialogue.

The failure of the contemporary curriculum is that while it

is wonderfully open to new ideas, it has not found a way of sustaining conversation on these novelties. If I were to take a lesson from Socrates, it would be not his skepticism but his persistence. Although he characterized himself as a gadfly he was not a giddy gadfly. He insisted on returning after every inconclusive argument to the same set of issues, with the belief that each inconclusive bout led forward dimly toward better vision. The modern curriculum is open enough, but college should be more than the Phil Donahue show with tuition. The scientific curriculum needs not only novel ideas and distinct challenges but continuing conversation. That is finally the secret of Science proper. It is not that scientists challenge old results; it is that they sustain a persistent conversation on certain issues until conclusions are reached. The earth really is more or less round.

The scientific university currently defines the territory for truth and knowledge; what is left undetermined is the life meaning (morality) of the modern course of study. Or: Need there be a moral purpose to higher education? The University of Chicago proclaims, "*Crescat scientia, vita excolatur*" ("Better things for better living through chemistry"). But is it so? The theme of science and student life is not easily resolved, and I doubt that it has a fully happy solution on any campus. Perhaps it is just improper to ask *universities* to solve the tasks of the spirit. Why should universities be expected to be a new religion, the older one having now fallen into some disrepair? Universities are marvelous, but they make lousy religions. Before addressing the spiritual state of the current campus—and the support of faith or fun at Academia U.—I want to examine in some detail how faculty and students mix and what they mix it up about: the liberal arts or whatever.

7

Sayonara, Mr. Chips

Any survey of *the* aspect of a college most desired by prospective students will indicate that it is "close faculty-student interaction." This observation can be quickly confirmed by looking at the advertising brochures of every one of the 3,300 colleges and universities of the land: Everybody promises close personal attention. So, if that is what is most desirable and if one can believe all that advertising, students will surely get their wish at whatever college of their choice.

There is a good deal of truth in all that advertising copy, but it is surprising that this should be so. Not because collegiate advertisers are dishonest, but because the trend lines of youth and professors and of their curricular coming together, sketched in the previous three chapters, would hardly suggest a comfortable community. To the extent that youth culture has defined itself as other than (if not "over and against") adulthood, why would one expect a ready mix with a thoroughly modern (and, by the way, adult) group of professional faculty? Helen

Horowitz's doleful Michigan student ("I'm having no fun") registers the disjunction of cultures. If there is a cause of the prevailing glums, it seems to rest on the divergence of faculty and student views on the common enterprise at hand. Close student-faculty interaction (or the lack of same) has not produced a happy community all round.

Let me be precise: there are still "bright college years with pleasures rife / The shortest gladdest years of life." No one has repealed youth—in fact, youth may never have been so much exalted as in the present day. What has changed—and what lies behind the Michigan student's cheerless remark—is the academic expectations of all those bright college years. In the days when the song was young, the colleges celebrated (Yale and its clones) were still determinedly into the old classical curriculum and the ministerial faculty of the day. Perhaps one imagines the ivy quad of yesterday as a cozy community of Chips and chaps. The record supports no such nostalgia.

Whatever the pleasures rife they were not at all involved with "close student-faculty relations." In his famous novel *Stover at Yale*, Owen Johnson recounted the life of John Humperdinck Stover during four years at Old Eli circa 1900. Over some 454 pages, Dink Stover goes through a series of adventures from freshman football to Tap Day. No once is it recounted that he even so much as meets a faculty member. The classical curriculum in its ministerial heyday produced a close community of students but not faculty *and* students. Demosthenes and other classical paragons of the curriculum were so distant from the needs of youth that students created their own community as a supplement to the aridity of the curriculum. First there were the literary societies of the early nineteenth century, where students could meet and discuss the perennial interests of young people: sex, politics, idealism. (We know this from the libraries of the societies and the records of their debates. Universities had no libraries to speak of. In 1829, the Princeton library added *one* book to its collection—and that one was a gift!) Then there came the fraternities, which taught students the social manners lacking in their ministerial drill masters. I once heard an ancient alumni officer at Princeton say that the most damaging blow to class spirit occurred when the old classical curriculum was abandoned. It was a tedious common task, like boot camp in the army. Getting through it was a common "pain in the brain" (another linguistic contribution from my daughters) so that the classes of '01, '02, '03, etc., had a camaraderie of combat never again attained. Bright college years indeed—but without the aid of faculty except as the common "enemy" or drill sergeant.

The virtue of the old classical curriculum for developing close *student* community was that it more or less left students alone. Not exactly, since it pestered their morals and perfected their grammar. But it did little to further some dominant youth interests: business career, athletics, pursuit of science, sex, exploring personal experience. The basis of student life and community was specifically and radically the concern of the student culture. One could say that the classical curriculum produced its own species of "youth culture." The difference between the youth culture of the classical curriculum and that of the contemporary scene was that the previous youth culture was adult-oriented while the present culture often seems self-enclosed. In Dink Stover's day youth was in opposition to the classical ancients, not the commercial adults.

In discussing the problems of contemporary fraternities, I have often suggested that fraternities were robbed of their traditional mission by the modern curriculum. Certainly their precursors, the literary societies, had long since been laid to rest when universities decided that books were to be purchased by the library. (The legendary Mark Hopkins, fraternity opponent and consummate teacher, also declared that one needed only one book in the Williams College library: the Bible.) The modern curriculum has become (at least in comparison to the one nineteenth-century students faced) overwhelmingly relevant. One may not learn the manners of the boardroom in "commercial studies," but one will certainly get up on the lingo. Science is everywhere; English departments explore the soul of youth from Jane Eyre to Holden Caulfield.

Add to the encroachment of relevant studies the profession-alized extracurriculum of sports, student affairs, personal coun-seling, and so on and on, and one might surmise that the nineteenth-century *student* agenda, the traditional world of youth, has been smothered in academic solicitude. College life is everything Dink Stover may have wanted—except it isn't fun any more, it's academic!

The previous discussion of professors indicates well enough what Professor Horowitz rightly concludes is the state of the contemporary college: the triumph of the clerks. The tone and temper of the contemporary educational establishment are set by the sense of serious professionalism that emerged out of the "scientific" revolution in the curriculum and the academic profession. Colleges and universities are intrinsically more se-rious places than in Stover's day. The irrelevance of the clas-sical curriculum matched the frivolity of student life. A relevant curriculum surrounded with career counselors and professional coaches seems to leave no room for freedom and fun. Enter Pink Floyd.

I have already suggested that close student-faculty relations in the old classical curriculum were illusory. Alums do recall a stern master or a kindly tutor, but in the manner of a tyran-nical drill sergeant or a benevolent orderly at boot camp. "Close"—that is, friendship—relations do not seem to have been the order of the day. The contemporary curriculum and its extras, with their seeming relevancy to life and career, should offer a more apposite meeting ground for faculty and students. But does it work? What are students *really* looking for behind those promises of "close student-faculty relations"?

Aristotle says in the first sentence of his *Metaphysics*, "All men by nature desire to know." Faculty often suggest that Aristotle never had to give a lecture immediately after lunch or he wouldn't have been so optimistic. Forgiving Aristotle his optimism (and unwitting sexism), this is a remarkable notion to contemplate: that there is a *natural* desire to know, that education is not something beaten into us by parents and ped-agogues. I believe in Aristotle and I quote him in a discussion of student-faculty interaction because the *closeness* of the interaction may be directly proportional to the urging of this (not always acknowledged) natural desire. (It is one natural desire that Freud didn't find in the id.) A student who desires "close student-faculty interaction" is absolutely certain to find it— and the very closest sort of it—under the promptings of the desire to know.

This may sound like a normal presidential platitude better reserved for commencement oratory, but it is fundamental in examining the community of a contemporary university. Faculty and students can be close and will be close, but the fully successful community is going to be on faculty turf—that is, academic; that is, classroom-related; that is, knowledge-desiring turf. The well-meaning notion that faculty and students are going to fraternize at the frats (sororize at the sororities) simply ignores different life interests, demands, and styles.

Back in the prehistoric 1950s, the Angevin Commission at Williams College recommended the abolition of fraternities because they were "an archaic nineteenth-century social structure which interfered with the natural community between faculty and students." The fraternities shrewdly countered that there was an archaic nineteenth-century social structure which interfered with the natural community of faculty and students—it was the faculty family. The answer was not to abolish fraternities but to return to a tradition of professorial celibacy. There is not now—and there is little evidence from history that there ever existed—a readily available social setting for faculty and students that is not laid out on some area of academic scenery. Thus, if students are seeking close student-faculty relations outside some larger version of the classroom setting, I believe they will be disappointed.

This judgment may sound too stringent, and it certainly applies differentially to different campus settings across the country. No one goes to a commuter college with much hope of socializing with faculty. Of course there are places where faculty and students play baseball after hours and where the departmental picnic is a jovial affair all the way round. Nevertheless, I would hold to the basic notion that today closeness is a function of classroom, not coffee klatch.

A student smitten with the "natural desire to know" who enrolls at even the most frigid research megaversity imaginable will inevitably find deep community with a faculty equally smitten with that desire. Community will grow over the test tubes, *then* over the beer mugs. Likewise, a student sullenly determined to resist education will be a bored outcast at the coziest of colleges. (Except that many a bored outcast devotes communal energy to some attendant collegiate activity. He or she has a good "college experience"—except, of course, he or she missed the college part.)

The actual problem of all universities and colleges in creating close faculty-student relations is that most students fall somewhere between, on one hand, Carlton Gadjusek's sixteen-year-old passion for particle physics and, on the other, absolute lay-aboutism. One need not fault the young or their culture too much for this state of affairs. At least in America we are permitted the luxury of the young "finding themselves." We do not force early choice and possible false passion on the young by insisting, like our European colleagues, that entering students pick their field of study at once. While in the process of finding the self, young people are likely to hedge all their classroom bets. Students matriculate at colleges but they do not necessarily enter the community of scholars.

The mix of yet-undecided youth with long-decided professors is perhaps the central problem of college experience for student and institution. It is the background concern that makes "closeness" a desired characteristic. Because undecided matriculants do not yet feel "close" to a subject of study they want someone to close the distance. Faculty are the obvious closers. The image of closing in the close atmosphere of a cozy seminar over coffee is not implausible. Almost every institution labors to create smallness in some or all of its teaching exercises. No one can miss some coziness in a collegiate experience, even at the megaversities. What strikes me, however, is that small is not necessarily beautiful. Coziness doth not a happy marriage make, as the divorce courts daily prove. My own sense is that it is not so much physical compactness as a communicated emotional closeness to the subject taught that counts. It is emotional commitment rather than smallness that makes for close student-faculty "feeling," and it is such commitment that defines great teaching.

If teaching is the road to close student-faculty relations, then applicants seeking community should certainly seek out great teaching institutions. And this is not difficult, since every college claims to be the very item sought. Are there great teaching institutions? I am inclined to believe the admissions rhetoric in this case. Yes. All of them and none of them.

It is extremely doubtful that there is some American university or college faculty that is the functional equivalent of the Royal Shakespeare Company. The first proof of this claim would be to note that there is no equivalent, in the training of teachers, to the Royal School of Dramatic Art. There are, of course, teacher-training programs, but they are for primary and secondary teachers. No one, seemingly, trains much to be a university teacher. I dare say that if you were to ask the faculty at the very best universities, the hottest colleges, the most prestigious places, whether they had ever had a course in teacher training they would collectively reply, "Thank God, never touch the stuff." (I happen to be an exception, since I spent a year as a Carnegie Research Fellow in University Teaching while at Chicago. It is not accidental that to make the whole idea palatable the word "research" was part of the title.)

Since there is no known training school of collegiate teaching, it would be surprising if the ability to teach was not randomly distributed across faculties according to the simple vagaries of human personality. To be sure, particular institutions might well select teaching types from the distribution. Here I can only rely on my personal observation to say that faculties I have dealt with as student, fellow faculty member, or senior administrator probably show no distinction in preponderance of teaching virtuosi than could be attributed to chance. If there is a variation toward Oscar-winning faculty, in my experience it tends to be where it might least be predicted—in the institutions, whether major universities or the most scholarly of the liberal arts colleges, that place a priority on research. At Brown University, a poll was conducted some years ago in which faculty rated colleagues for their excellence as scholars and researchers; students were at the same time asked to grade faculty for their prowess as teachers. There was a significant correlation between excellence in research and excellence in teaching. I am inclined to believe that these results have general validity.

Only general validity, of course. There are always very notable exceptions. Some researchers should be confined to arcane conferences of specialists; brilliant teachers who have scant interest in publishing can flourish (though it is not easy to make a career in teaching at any advanced level without some measure of advancing scholarship in one's field).

Not only do I not believe that physical proximity is a guarantor of "closeness," I call any college-graduate reader as witness that much of the "great teaching" he or she experienced was inversely proportional to the square of the distance to the student. A bit of reflection will reveal, I conjecture, that many of the great teachers whom one recalls were great *lecturers*. Frankly, they were people who could put on a show. Bernard M. W. Knox intoning Greek verse to an uncomprehending class of five hundred was one of the accepted great teaching moments in my days at Yale. Later, Vince Scully, teaching architecture, knocked them in the aisles by the hundreds. If one goes back in history to "great teachers"—William Lyon Phelps, Dexter Perkins, Jinx Harbison (I name from memory and institutional loyalty faculty known both generally and locally as great teachers)—these folks were one and all "actors," who dramatized their subject in well-developed lectures.

It is puzzling that memory can recall great lecturers when the paradigm carried about for great teaching is of an intimate discussion. Great lecturing is far from the whole of great teaching. One would scarcely want to go to an institution which offered only an array of performers. Finally the student needs dialogue with an intelligent and concerned teacher—but it is paradoxical that this dedicated soul is likely not to be remembered, when Herbert Alyea and his Ping-Pong ball lecture on nuclear fusion are vividly recalled.

Close student-faculty interaction is complex if not enigmatic. The most assured ground for closeness is common intellectual interest—after all, faculty have dedicated their lives to psychology or topology, for all that they can play a good game of racquetball in after hours. It is a pleasant reassurance to an apprehensive freshman that the professor smiles and shows other signs of common humanity, but there is work to be done. If the student doesn't want the work, the smile will not blossom into friendship.

"Close student-faculty interaction" may be another of those terms that need to be translated from Studentese. While the notion has its absolute validity and is, in fact, one of the most precious outcomes of the academic endeavor, it can be used—like all noble ideas—to mask its opposite. Recall that what is being sought is *academic* community, close *faculty*-student friendship. It is easy enough to gloss over "academic" and "faculty" and believe that simple community and friendship are at issue. Whatever the warmth of the collegiate prose, no one is advertising, "Come to Lite College for the fun and frolic."

I will yield to no one when it comes to being (having been) an anxious applicant. My dearest wish was to go to a small denominational college managed by folks whom I knew from attending summer camp. The principal reason was sheer terror about my ability to do college-level work. I felt that the same folks who had taught me canoeing would certainly not overstrain my academic capacity. Fortunately, my father persuaded me otherwise. (This is probably why I encourage parental persuasion in college choice.)

"Small and close" will not necessarily create community of faculty and student; finally the student has to buy the curricular product. Buying into the physicists' discipline will surely create the greatest intimacies among the quarks and other strange particles. That is probably well understood. But it returns us to the puzzle first enunciated, that all colleges (well, almost all) proclaim something more as their special trade. That something more is usually labeled "liberal arts." How does one close with a prof on that turf?

8

Snarks, Boojums, and Liberal Arts

Judging by the behavior of college-seekers, one would conclude that "liberal arts" is a definitive Snark—the beast madly pursued by Lewis Carroll's explorers in "The Hunting of the . . ." The problem with the Snark is that absolutely no one seems able to describe the thing accurately at all. Nevertheless, a "liberal-arts education" appears, on the basis of consumer behavior, to be a most desirable item. Whole institutions describe themselves as liberal-arts colleges, and even the most complex of universities will proudly boast that they have not lost sight of "the importance of liberal-arts education." The previous chapters on modern professors and their curricular tastes should raise some skepticism about this catalogue enthusiasm for the liberal arts. *The* liberal arts flourished in the time of Church Gothic architecture; do they really survive in the Collegiate Imitation Gothic campus? (Yale Gothic is circa 1925, after all.)

The easiest way to define liberal arts is to note what it (evidently) is not. Students with clear-cut professional or career

aims seldom think of themselves as liberal-arts students. En-
gineers and pre-meds do not seek the Snark. By process of
elimination, "liberal arts" conforms to what a Gallup Poll
might turn up: "liberal arts" usually means "undecided." If an
applicant announces that he or she plans to study liberal arts,
that usually signals that the mind has not been made up.
Unfortunately, no institution that I knew of has billed itself as
an "undecided college." One would also wish that so dignified
a term as "liberal arts" signified something more than an academic holding pattern maintained while awaiting a stroke of
grace or accident of fate to point a life direction.

The genuinely undecided may in fact be indicating a desire
for a *general* education, as contrasted to some visible specialization like aeronautical engineering or pre-veterinary studies.
Truly there is something "general" about liberal arts, but "general" seems a rather weak content for four years of tuition. I
would not recommend telling the corporate recruiter, "I am
a generalist, you see. Not one of those chaps who knows accounting or chemistry or South American history. No, really
a generalist."

Worse yet, there are insuperable institutional problems for
the genuine generalist. Nobody (hardly anybody) offers a B.A.
in generalizing. If a student really wants a general education
he or she faces general frustration. Almost every student finally
is required to major in something and, to confuse matters,
most specialize in one of the liberal arts. So much for one sort
of generality.

If the undecided generalist is finally forced to decide on a
major in something that the college will label a liberal art,
where has he or she arrived? In truth, at a historical hangover.
The longest ancestral line of liberal arts goes back to the Greeks
(again), when the "liberal" arts were those thought worthy of
study by free citizens. Free, in contrast to slaves and menial
laborers. The free arts contrasted with the knacks and skills of
what we now would call "technical" trades. A trireme maker
knew something, but this practical know-how was not consid-

ered fit for the free. Liberal arts were for those freed from the necessity of having practical skills; the liberal arts were, in short, the activity of a leisured class. The word "school" comes from the Greek word for leisure, *skole*. Aristotle traces the origin of free (nonpractical) study to Egyptian priests, who, because they did not perform labor, were able to invent pure mathematics.

A second historical line for liberal arts is found in the origin of universities. The Greeks invented the notion of arts for free men, but they did not coin the term "liberal arts" or create the social institution we call universities. The *artes liberales* were formalized during the Middle Ages, along with the notion of the university itself.

There were seven *artes liberales*, divided in two parts: the quadrivium of astronomy, music, mathematics, and geometry, and the trivium of logic, rhetoric, and grammar. Unfortunately for Snark-hunters these tradiational *artes liberales* either appear today as minor subparts of something else, or are not now what they once were, or are not taught at all. Few colleges teach rhetoric in any recognizable form; logic is subdiscipline of philosophy; and music as part of the quadrivium dealt with mathematical proportions, not lessons on the hautbois and viol. When there is some clear continuance of *artes liberales* recognizable in the modern curriculum, it is not generally recognized as a liberal art. Astronomy is a noble endeavor, but not normally associated with the liberal arts. In fact, few people think of the natural sciences as liberal *arts* at all. Science and "art" are supposedly different directions in life and study. (A scrupulous college-president friend always referred to his college's curriculum as "the liberal arts and the liberal *sciences*." "Liberal" may well be applied to the sciences *honoris causa*, but it is not current terminology.) A modern philosopher of the collegiate curriculum reviewing remnants of the *artes liberales* at Contemporary U. might well conclude that their historical critics were correct: The trivium is trivia, and well enough left alone.

So far it seems that "liberal arts" may mean "undecided" or

"general" (about something or other), or "what one does with free time" (the twentieth century extracurriculum?) or a set of seven semiarchaic studies. A last piece for this curricular conundrum: As was discussed at some length in the account of the romance of American higher education, American higher education has differentiated itself from the European tradition by accepting some species of moral or spiritual mission for collegiate education. This too is part of the historical hangover denoted by our affection for the liberal arts. William Jennings Bryan said he cared more about the Rock of Ages than the age of rocks. So did many a pious nineteenth-century college president and his faculty. A university that eschewed the liberal arts would seem to be selling its ethical inheritance for a mess of professional pottage.

The list of contemporary American "moral" liberal arts is, of course, not at all consonant with the medievals'. One notes at once that mathematics is very much a medieval liberal art, while almost no one seems to regard it as such in an American context. (The only moral lesson most American students believe that they get from calculus is endurance.) For Americans, liberal arts are supposed to be value laden, so our quadrivium (expanded) includes literature, art, history, philosophy, and probably sociology, anthropology, and other social sciences, provided they are not too "scientific."

The overall conclusion, then, is that American liberal-arts education seems to be a course of study in some sort of values (more or less) and that this is (somehow) tied up with the general sort of things that anyone (more or less) ought to learn. This definition is 2 percent clearer than Lewis Carroll's description of the Snark; what should we make of it?

"Liberal arts" aim in its woozy way at something deep and fundamental about what is *higher* in higher education. In the long run it turns out to be some uneasy amalgam or mush of the arts of free persons, *artes liberales*, elevated theory, and moral earnestness. Higher education should be freeing, general, moral—and high. How does it work?

Freedom

All real education liberates. "Ye shall know the truth and the truth shall make you free." Knowing the truth about a good weld is liberating, if you want to be "free" to fasten hunks of steel. Education that fails to free the learner we re gard as no education at all: It is learning bad habits, having traumatic experience, which cripple rather than create. We may bring up our children so badly that they become psychotics, but it would be very odd to say, "I am educating Junior to be a paranoid." Freedom is an essential characteristic of what counts as education and a necessary aim of any curriculum.

That essential sense of "free" is present in anything that we call education, but there is a higher sense of freedom in higher ed. Our most advanced colleges and universities differentiate themselves from technical-training institutes by a further consideration of freedom. Any art (Greek *techne*) frees human beings from some slavery to nature or ignorance. Advanced education at the university level, however, imitates the Greek notion of free studies (without, I hope, imitating its social stratification). University education seeks knowledge for its own sake, not for any immediate usefulness in making a laser or a living. Physics has had immense practical consequences in the modern world, from redefining our environment to restructuring the nature of global conflict, but it would be eminently worthwhile as a pursuit if none of that had occurred. There *is* a natural desire to know.

One of my favorite stories from the lives of famous philosophers is a tale about Bertrand Russell. Well on into his late eighties Russell attended a lecture on astrophysics. The lecturer was discussing events in one of the distant galaxies—events that had, of course, occurred millions of years previously. After the lecture Russell commented to the speaker, "Isn't it wonderful to know things like that." Galactic events eons ago could have had small practical significance even to an octogenarian philosopher. Russell was imitating Aristotle—not a posture he generally favored—by registering the natural delight in knowledge for its own sake.

The fundamental freedom of the liberal arts is the freedom of understanding before (or beyond) practicality. University studies are in some large sense finally interested in theory. We not only want to be able to know how but to know *why*. In this sense of free (non-know-how) understanding almost everything in almost every college of note is "liberal arts," French literature and astrophysics alike. Even engineering and professional studies, as pursued in university settings, contain a deep concern for fundamental theory that goes beyond simply getting something done. We may know that pill Z cures disease Y, but we want to know why this is so, and so mere practice turns to theory.

The liberal-arts-as-freedom theory has much to "dis-recommend" it in the context of American higher education. That most American of philosophers, John Dewey, thought Aristotle had started the philosophy of education on a bad note with his distinction between technical practice and "free" theory. For Dewey, education should be reinserted in practical contexts. It wasn't speculative philosophers who invented modern science—it was practical folk, who *worked* with the things of this earth and so discovered their secrets.

This high-road Deweyian critique of arts that have liberated themselves from practical life may also echo the more mundane worry of the parent whose offspring is studying some undoubted and impractical liberal art—like Aristotelian philosophy. For all that "liberal arts" has a glow to it in the admissions brochure, the minute the student is admitted to a rarefied liberal-arts institution everyone may begin a scramble to discover the most practical possible liberal art.

The resolution of the quarrel between immediate pragmatism and utter theory was revealed in the initial discussion of cow and bull. Immediately practical education cows along; it fits the first job but lacks escape routes to a second—and to advancement. Theory gives one a grasp beyond the immediate routine; it makes learning the next task that much easier. Since

Americans change jobs, homes and, more recently, spouses on a short cycle, some broader understanding of work, place, and persons is utterly practical.

Generality

Seeking *theory* also explains the urge to generality embedded in the yearning for liberal arts. Having a theory about cancer gives a most general picture of the disease beyond its immediate specified forms. A further level of generality should be noted, however, since it relates to the trivium of the *artes liberales*. If there is one insistent complaint about contemporary colleges it is that they have abandoned the trivium. The newspaper headlines may not *sound* like that, but the repeated condemnation of graduates who cannot read, write, speak, or argue is nothing more or less than a complaint that they have not mastered grammar, rhetoric, and logic.

If there is a problem with the *artes liberales* in the modern university it is not that they are not taught but that they are taught everywhere. Like the famous M. Jourdain, who was startled to discover that he had been speaking prose all his life, students (and faculty) may be surprised to discover that grammar, rhetoric, and logic are all over the curriculum, from Freshman Comp to Chem Lab Reports. Of course, when one speaks prose unconsciously one may take too little conscious trouble to speak it well. Recent emphasis on "writing" in college exercises may be regarded as a mild effort to do consciousness-raising on the trivium.

Morality

If *artes liberales* are all over the curriculum and thus disappear into ubiquity, the same might be said for the last of the liberal-arts traditions in America. Morality is there, but diffused toward disappearance.

Bad enough that American pragmatism and American parents worry about the rarefication of free theory; the liberated notion of study also sits uncomfortably with the moral urges of traditional American liberal-arts pedagogy. If John Dewey disliked the pure theory of the ancients, so did those college faculties that happily suspended classes in the classics to provide time for moral revival. The clash between the ancient tradition of "free theory" and the specific American urge to practicality (moral or careerist) is at the heart of many of the issues that confront colleges and universities in making up their curricular minds and selling their minds to students, supporters, and society at large. Should society support free theoretical studies—maybe physics but what about French linguistics? If there is to be a "practical" content to the liberal arts, what moral message should be chosen? Or should one abandon moral practicality for sheer careerist praticality and teach Business English and Calculus for Clerks?

It seems relatively easy to discover the ivory-tower university into free theory; the moral side of the liberal-arts tradition is not so easily perceived today, despite all the commencement oratory regarding same. A semirealistic appraisal of the academic scene might conclude that theory had taken over completely. Not quite.

The old liberal-arts college, which was invented in the fervor of the church, was very straightforward about its moral and spiritual instruction. Citing another Lewis Carroll creation, the Duchess: The old curriculum always said, "And the moral of *that* is . . ." Modern-day liberal-arts institutions lay claim to moral tradition, but somewhat in the spirit of the believer who described himself as a "lapsed liberal Unitarian." The *content* of the American "humanities" is chock-full of moral and spiritual ideas. Who can read *War and Peace* or the history of modern France without coming across striking moral issues and persuasive ethical views? What will not come across, in most liberal-arts courses, is any extensive articulation of some set of values purveyed by the curriculum. There may be some such consensus, but at most places it is distinctly understated. When I studied literary criticism at Yale it had a determinedly Christian cast, which no one would have denied but which no one would have particularly proclaimed either. It is not difficult to discover liberal-arts areas that are determinedly Maoist or Marxist, or as "Christian" as the Yale New Critics. It is just that folks don't brag about it in the brochures.

An exception to "unarticulated morality" in the curriculum has arisen from feminist and ethnic critics. To these commentators, the morality of the curriculum is perfectly evident and needs to be exposed for its falsity, perversity, narrowness, machismo, and so on. These criticisms are of great value, I believe, not necessarily because they are always correct but because they demand some self-conscious appraisal of the moral value of the course of study. The stridency of the debate is, I believe, directly proportional to the lack of recent practice in self-consciously addressing the moral issues of the liberal arts.

It is instructive in this context to recognize that some colleges maintain highly articulated moral convictions within the curriculum and outside it. Wheaton College in Illinois is a clearcut, no-nonsense Evangelical college. Student life is a remnant of days gone by elsewhere: mandatory chapel, compulsory Bible-study courses. No alcohol, smoking, or improper coeducationalizing. Wheaton attracts top-ranked National Merit Scholars and ranks among the top dozen or so colleges in the nation in percentage of graduates who go on to take doctoral degrees. Wheaton rightly regards itself as "the Harvard of Evangelical Protestantism." Having taught students who transferred from Wheaton, I conclude that the Evangelical character of the curriculum is a powerful educational force. Admittedly, my students had transferred because they found the life too restrictive—as some certainly would—but it was clear that the conviction behind the curriculum and the institution was a continuous and serious challenge to active and creative thought.

While the American liberal arts are rooted in a moral tradition, only a rather special set of the new youth are likely to choose the Wheaton model for developing a set of moral convictions. The prevailing college ethos seems to be that the liberal arts, while they should have moral content, should not be *too* clear about it. It was the tepid quality of the modern, liberated liberal arts that caused the late Chancellor Robert Maynard Hutchins of the University of Chicago to refer to the Ivy League universities and their ilk as "finishing schools." It was his hope to revivify, through the Great Books, the "moral" liberal arts in a context beyond the church. The University of Chicago replaced Wheaton's compulsory Bible study with a required four-year curriculum covering thinkers from Plato to the present. The greats were forced to argue with one another and with the students.

One could probably construct a continuum of colleges from Wheaton to Wherever on the basis of degrees of self-conscious value orientation in the curriculum. The values may be decidedly religious—but this is rare these days—they may be embodied in the greats (as at St. John's in Annapolis); or the school may have some partial package of integrated studies, as in the Columbia two-year General Studies program. On the whole, however, most colleges and universities are on the Wherever side of the curriculum. Values abound in the "liberal arts," but they are not bound to any Gospel or greats.

If one were to take a census, then, of the liberal-arts urge in the contemporary college, Greek "theory" prevails over American "gospel." In the direct teaching of ethics Greek theory again prevails. Ethics, as taught in most philosophy departments in the country, is not concerned with improving the behavior of the students. Ethics is most often "meta-ethics," that is, the consideration of what it would mean to say that some action was "right" or "good." (You may have your own views about whether abortion or surrogate parenting is good, but what does the word "good" mean in whatever choice is made?)

It would be simple if one could just leave well enough alone and conclude that modern universities are really very modern indeed. Modern studies are theoretical and the American moral curriculum is gradually fading into history. People may again say that theory is trivial, but the free scholar knows that it is the proper delight of the human mind. If practical folk won't buy these liberal arts they are mere mechanicals! Aristotle wins again.

Alas, morality is not easily abandoned. Pure theory has its own moral purities. One cannot lie in the palace of true theory, and one needs the courage of conviction. American education is deeply committed to (or inextricably mired in) the (moral) liberal arts. As a University president I am committed to (or mired in) making speeches on that head on occasions beyond measure. Nevertheless, the moral mission of the modern scientific university, in contrast to that of its religiously enthused predecessors, is exceedingly difficult to specify. The last chapter of this section will do what can be done to find a suppressed spirituality for our scientific studies.

9

Student Hero:
An Essay in Ontology

Duming my duty as dean of dropouts, there were constant meetings between the various deans and the assemblage of psychiatrists, psychological counselors, chaplains, and others professionally concerned with the mental and spiritual condition of the student body and its soul. After one protracted dissection of the psychic state of the campus, my boss dean remarked in a mixture of bafflement and exasperation, "I can't understand all this fuss about 'Who am I?' When I was in college in the thirties my only concern was 'What job can I get?' "

The boss dean's bafflement remains. College is certainly a step in career preparation—sometimes that is the only conscious purpose for the bother of attending. But, in many and intricate ways both planned and promised, spontaneous and sporadic, exhilarating and exasperating, the college years for young people are a time to discover a persona as well as a profession. If these two tasks were only accidentally linked there would be no great need for universities to attend to them. Few colleges believe that dental hygiene is a necessary corollary to algebraic topology. Whether there actually is a connection between self and study, the fact is that colleges and universities often make their biggest pitch to the personal. Personal *experience* is the central myth of American higher education; assaying the myth properly ends the first section of this book.

Linkage of the personal and educational certainly exists, for good or ill. All my dropouts of yesteryear were fleeing educational opportunity because some personal need or neurosis made study intolerable. In Dad's day the choice of profession *was* the choice of persona (or vice versa). In the thoroughly modern university, profession and personal style seem to have become separate issues. Answering the question "Who am I?" may remain a psychic need of sophomores, but if the issue is addressed it will be in the counseling service of the medical center, not (at least not obviously) in the "scientific" curriculum.

I am a metaphysician by trade (there is a practical career choice!), so the mundane problem of curricular career and (student) life gets translated into the ontological distinction between Doing and Being: What shall I do? What shall I be? The late Walker Percy invented a fictional "ontological lapsometer" to measure the emptiness (lack of *being* who I am) in modern life. In this summation chapter I will apply the lapsometer to college life in order to dissect the "ontological lapses of the modern university." (The study of Being is called ontology; this is a useful word for making a social impression. Parent: "We are considering the ontological implications of Jane attending Stanford.")

On the matter of Doing, modern universities are splendid indeed; on Being they and the society seem to be in a continuing crisis. The split between Doing and Being is particularly acute for college students, since it is at that time of life that who-am-I-and-what-shall-I-do emerge so insistently into consciousness. Failing the ontological lapsometer test means flunking Fun 101.

It is not accidental that modern philosophers who worry

about the Being of this or that often write novels (Sartre, Camus, Gabriel Marcel, Iris Murdoch). These anguishing ontologists seek the density of the person himself or herself and nothing short of the density of a replicated life will convey the message. I would have preferred to write a novel about collegegoing as a guide to student Being. I have been deterred from this urge by talent (lacking) and precedent (bad)—academic novels are almost uniformly as boring, misleading, and mythic as college catalogues.

The inadequacy of academic novels can be cited as evidence of the persistent inadequacy of student life. That academic novels are so depressingly bad should seem strange. The great critic George Saintsbury, writing in 1898, thought the student an ideal subject for fiction. (Forgive the reference to young *men*; the story is surely as plausible for young women.)

> There can be, or should be, few passages in life with greater capabilities than that when a man is for the first time almost his own master, for the first time wholly arbiter of whatsoever sports and whatsoever studies he shall pursue, and when he is subjected to local, historical, and other influences, sensual and supersensual, such as might not only "draw three souls out of a weaver" but infuse something like soul into the stupidest and most graceless of boys.

George Santayana seemed closer to the mark, however, when he wrote to a friend: "To judge from my experience I should say that Harvard yields no good material for fiction." Despite the fact that Santayana's own novel, *The Last Puritan*, is something of a refutation of his claim, the literary record tends to confirm the emptiness of the college experience as recorded in the American academic novel. The novels in turn are as bad as the experience described. Whether college really is as empty as the novelists proclaim or whether bad novels show bad perception of a deep experience may be the real question to be addressed.

There have been lots of academic novels even by great masters. The very first college novel was written by none other than Nathaniel Hawthorne. His first novel, *Fanshawe*, published in 1828, was set at Harley College (a thinly disguised Bowdoin, from which Hawthorne graduated in 1825. Hawthorne later wished to repress the effort; his literary taste was impeccable.) Hawthorne set one of the standard novelistic condemnations of college in his depiction of the childless, infertile president of Fanshawe. The sterility of college continually impresses novelists. By the time Professor John Lyons wrote his study of collegiate novels in the mid-1960s, there were 171 extant efforts. Almost all of the academic novels are eminently forgettable—with the possible exception of F. Scott Fitzgerald's *This Side of Paradise*—and almost all are uniformly dismissive of "academics."

Reading through a selection of academic novels might well lead to the conclusion that there is something essentially wrong with the whole collegiate idea. Most academic novels are comic, and this is hardly accidental. The academy as the claimant on *lux*, *veritas*, and other large notions is a prime target for the sharp-eyed critics. Pretentiousness can be unmasked only where one reaches for something of high value. The distinguished don, so severe in scholarship, caught in sexual silliness, is an eminent figure of fun. Only the church might offer a better venue for puncturing pomposities than the academy does, but since Trollope no one seems to have been that much interested in bishops.

Not all academic novels about failed ideals are funny. Thomas Wolfe wrote extensively about his experiences at North Carolina and Harvard. For Wolfe, the academy was a place of pedantry, dandyism, and intellectual snobbery. Wolfe's review of Harvard et al. is echoed by such high thinkers as Emerson and such modest ideologues as Dink Stover. Emerson lamented "the meek young men who grow up in libraries," and Dink thinks that the real lessons of life are not in the books but in the playing fields and prairies of his Nebraskan friend, Tom Regan.

The fictional failure of colleges seems to be confirmed by the actual historical record. Classical authors didn't fill the ambitious lives of the young men of the late nineteenth century, so they went ahead and invented the fraternity movement without bothering to seek the permission of the ministerial presidential authority. (The authority disapproved.) Contemporary student argot divides life-at-college between "academics" and, well, everything else, which is where reality and "fun" seem to abide. It is not insignificant that the various guidebooks rate social life and food as solemnly as they do "academics." One should not go to college and miss life itself! The extracurriculum outpaces the "rational" curriculum in the "reality" game—a fascinating comment on the scientific curricular philosophy of the day. (Physics is unreal; football is real life! There must be some mistake.)

Personal doubt about *real* education in college *classrooms* has a strong American flavor. European attitudes can differ sharply from the American assumption that true value in life or art occurs extracurricularly. In 1832 the redoubtable Mrs. Frances Trollope published *Domestic Manners of the Americans,* her celebrated and caustic tour of the United States. She relates a conversation with an American gentleman she met at a party:

> At length he named an American artist . . . and after declaring him the equal to Lawrence . . . he added "and what is more, madam, he is perfectly self taught."
> I prudently took a few moments before I answered; for the equalling our immortal Lawrence to a vile dauber stuck in my throat. . . . At last I remarked on the frequency with which I had heard the phrase *self taught* used, not as an apology, but as positive praise.

Despite all the American effort and apparent enthusiasm for higher education, there remains the deep suspicion that the really real is self-taught. Curriculum remains trivium; the real education occurs in Nebraska or downtown Boston, and though one may learn cost accounting in class, "who I am" is learned with Dink Stover in the Princeton game.

Much has been made in this book about the character given to *American* higher education by its denominational origins. Denominationalism has disappeared or diffused on almost all campuses—even at those with overt religious sponsorship. The diminution of denominationalism is the result of economic pressure (there never are enough Methodists at hand to fill the class) and academic professionalism. In denominational days the matter of "who I am" was the essence of the enterprise. There was the classical/Christian curriculum, which, while it did little for knowledge of science, made much of heroism. The twin pillars of the classical curriculum were literary style and life-style. One was tutored incessantly on the elegance of Latin and the bravery of Aeneas. George Washington was "father of his country," not only because of his heroism but because the phrase is a direct translation of the Augustan *pater patriae*. If classical heroism did not suffice there was the Christian heroism preached on Sunday and enhanced in the annual revival. The mission of the college was the total life of the young person. Cardinal Newman's ideal of the "Christian gentleman" could serve broadly as the aim of higher education everywhere in the nineteenth century college.

"Who am I?" was a question for which the Christian College of the day had a ready answer. Persona was no ultimate Socratic ideal or underground Freudian mystery. Being a Christian clergyperson did not suit the place-getting fraternity student, circa 1880, but fraternities were as much interested in personal style as the ministerial president was. Dink Stover may not have attended any classes at Yale (as far as the literary text indicates) but he picked up the basic collegiate lesson of being a hero and a gentleman. The higher education that encased Horatio Alger ambition was finally concerned with "Who am

I?" In the case of the education of women, persona clearly overcame profession in earlier days. There were so few professions open to women that persona was the sole function. The importance of "life-style" as the fundamental educational expectation overflowed its basic denominational setting. (I much dislike the term "life-style" to describe a decision for religious or moral commitment, but it is a term of art these days. William Sloane Coffin once remarked: "Next time they start talking about 'life-style,' why don't you ask about 'life content'!)

For all sorts of the most complex reasons, both good and bad, the conjunction of Being and Doing in America and its colleges has been loosened if not wholly broken. We lack the general moral consensus of our Victorian ancestors. One's minister may now be a woman, divorced, homosexual—or all three—and that is accepted. In achieving a much-needed tolerance in society, in opening up place and privilege to the previously excluded, the society has advanced morally. On the other hand, it makes the problem of "Who am I?" overwhelmingly individual. One cannot pick a life-style from the rack of career options or derive it from an ambient moral atmosphere.

(Actually, I suspect that life-style is even more determined by ambience these days than it was in Victoria's reign. The more one breaks down preformed life-styles of class, gender, and profession the more anxious the choice of style becomes. The result is homogenization, as one looks to the crowd for cues. In the modern college undergraduate society, homogeneity is urgently advanced under the slogan "Do your own thing." In my days as dropout dean, a frequent complaint of droppers-out was that students were too much "the same." This phrase could *always* be translated: "Why aren't there more students here like me?")

The de-denominationalizing of the colleges (which has been going on alongside of, as a cause of, and because of the division of job and life) has left higher education with few clear institutional instruments for practicing ontology on students. During the 1960s I wrote an article entitled "Bring Back Compulsory Chapel." At Middlebury we were consistently ad-

monished by concerned students to "take a stand" on the Viet-
nam War. There are lots of academic-freedom problems in
colleges' taking official moral and political stands—but I
pointed out that even if we were to take a stand, it wasn't clear
where we would read the proclamation. When Archibald Cox
was fired by President Nixon, Derek Bok took the highly unusual step for a modern university president of requisitioning
the Sunday pulpit at the Harvard Chapel to welcome Mr. Cox
back to Harvard. The old compulsory chapel service was a
place where college authorities could "take a stand." In the
1930s at Middlebury, the then president took a stand in the
compulsory chapel on the European war. He told the students
it was "our war"; they were deeply offended.

Compulsory chapel was a hangover of denominational days
and one will not see its like again. But if there is no chapel,
no set of classical life-styles, if we have the reticence of academic freedom and broad moral tolerance, in what way can
modern universities address personal life and value? Selling
stocks in tobacco or apartheid is a one-day symbol, not a constant preaching. On alternate weekdays, I am tempted to believe that the university *as university* should simply not worry
about moral choice, spiritual value and "Who am I, anyway?"
There are courses in history, anthropology, literature, philosophy, and so on, that consider such questions—but, one
assumes, with appropriate academic diffidence. Individual faculty and students may take a stand, but institutions do not
preach from compulsory chapels or required moral curricula.
(Consider the apprehension expressed about having required
courses on "racism" or "sexism." The fear is that such courses
won't "examine the subject" but preach a doctrine. Despite
the fact that one supposes every university citizen abhors racism, "indoctrination" is abhorred even more. But indoctri-
nating [the Ten Commandments] was the main task of the
denominational college.)

Unfortunately for my dreams of rinsing out ontology once
and for all from the curriculum, any teaching—even and especially with distance and diffidence—presents a life-style. Dif-

fidence on the part of the institution is precisely what annoys artists like Wolfe and protesters galore. Academic profession-alism appears as academic pedantry to souls concerned with life at large beyond the quad. It is intriguing, of course, that academic novelists and political organizers alike should be so annoyed at just these institutions. Academic novelists may scorn classroom goings-on, but it is significant that they use this setting for a tale of coming-of-age or rebellion. One would not set such stories so well in a shoe factory or telephone-supply warehouse. You need to have an institution of pro-claimed aspiration. There has to be a Holy Grail. Universities may no longer have a dogmatic gospel to preach, but some certain and vague Ideal yet to come is on their promissory note. Artists and agitators sense the Ideal and call in the promise. "But that is not what we meant at all. Not at all." Well, what did you mean?

While artists and agitators protest the university's failure to meet the grand Ideal, to give the fullness that life demands and the admissions brochure promised, the more routine sep-aration of curriculum and the full life is registered by the supposed funlessness of the academic scene. "Fun" implies "fullness"; no one has "fun" in a fit of diffidence, while preoc-cupied, or when having second thoughts. "Fun" may not name the deepest density of life, but it points to something whole and entire. If students today aren't having "fun," lack of ac-ademic-ontological density may be the root cause.

I turn, then, to a commentary on modern college life as full or as running on empty. Despite all its novelistic critics, the life of the academy is not without resource for fullness. No one has expressed this more poignantly than a novelist not noted for applauding the academic setting: Philip Roth. In this scene from *The Professor of Desire*, a hapless Professor Keppish writes a letter to his junior class in literature:

Dear Students:

I love teaching literature. I am rarely ever so con-tented as when I am here with my pages of notes,

and my marked-up texts, and with people like your-
selves. To my mind there is nothing quite like the
classroom in all of life. Sometimes when we are
in the midst of talking—when one of you, say, has
pierced with a single phrase right to the heart of
the book at hand—I want to cry out, "Dear friends,
cherish this!" Why? Because once you have left
here people are rarely, if ever, going to talk to you
or listen to you the way you talk and listen to one
another and to me in this bright and barren little
room. Nor is it likely that you will easily find opportunities elsewhere to speak without embarrass-
ment about what has mattered most to men as
attuned to life's struggles as were Tolstoy, Mann,
and Flaubert. I doubt that you know how very
affecting it is to hear you speak thoughtfully and
in all earnestness about solitude, illness, longing,
loss, suffering, delusion, hope, passion, love, terror, corruption, calamity, and death . . . moving
because . . . oddly and sadly, this may be the last
occasion you will ever have to reflect in any sustained and serious way upon the unrelenting forces
with which in time you will all contend, like it or
not.

The normal novelistic assumptions of full and empty are
reversed. It is the dossiers of the students that are empty of
the experiences to which the great novelists give full expression.

Arguing for the fullness of Keppish's classroom is simply not
sufficient, however, to establish ontology in the modern
scientific curriculum. The contemporary humanities curriculum shadows classical greats and may attend to "Who am I?"
with passion—especially since it is so uncertain what Professor Keppish's literary students will *do* with their B.A. in
English. The fundamental question is "the fullness quotient"
within the scientific curriculum overall and the university of

disciplines it has created—that institution which replaced definitively the classical curriculum and the denominational college?

If students enter with glee into "academics" they will, of course, find fulfillment and fun in philology. If they stand aside from the academics of academics, life at college may depend on the quality of local shopping malls. That answer is fundamental but rather too easy. It suggests that the only full lesson to be learned at the modern university is to become a full professor. Personally, I find the professorial life deeply satisfying, but I would not demand it of students as the single key to the Grails of reality and fun.

To extricate the ontological possibilities of Thoroughly Modern U., I offer an arbitrary, somewhat accurate, mnemonic triplet of concepts that compare the older denominational-classical college with its modern scientific successor. The life virtues and personal vices of the old and new curricula (classical versus scientific) might be set out as follows: the virtues of the older style are Classics, commitment, and community. For the scientific curriculum I suggest tentativeness, tolerance, and tenacity. These concepts are linked in each curricular philosophy.

The central value of the classical curriculum is the very idea of the classic. "Classic" denotes something that is better than the norm, a model of the type, a heroic form of emulation. A world that did not believe in the idea of the classic would be one without a sense of better or worse in anything from motor cars to moral action. The classic ideal may be hero or heroine, the "white man's burden" or the "noble savage." The *form* of the classic is the same, though one may come to regard some "classics" as classic blunders. A world without classics would be not only bad but boring—a plain plane. The idea that there are classics creates a community based on the standards of the classic. The classic is a cause to which all may repair. Lacking the classic, it is each for his or her own and it doesn't make any difference anyhow. Finally, "classic" suggests commitment. Heroes are highlighted and one commits to a heroic life or literature.

The vices of the classical curriculum are brought out by the alternative values of the scientific course of study. Tentativeness may not seem a ready virtue, but in a world of dogma, fanaticism, and false heroes it is a genuine moral advance. The young ought not be pressed too soon into commitment, whether to careers in plastics or some other synthetic life choice. (Youth culture is ambiguous on the matter of commitment. At times it seems that the message is "Bop along," but at other times there appears an urgency for commitment to cause, or to sex or whatever. Tentativeness can be well advised for the young.)

Tentativeness leads to the second ringing and unambiguous virtue of the new style of learning: tolerance. Lacking the assurance of assured classics or revealed religion, the new university curriculum is broadly tolerant. New and important voices are heard beyond a raft of—to tell the truth—dusty Romans. (No slur on the great ones, but a lot of second-rate speech writers made it to the canon.) When one doesn't know *for sure*, then it is important to be tolerant of other opinions.

At this juncture in arraying scientific virtue, the classicists counter: Maybe tolerance and tentativeness are virtues up to a point, but if they become the style of life (as well as learning) what happens to commitment and community? I may be tentative about muons, but how can I be tentative about being alive? If the *life lesson* of the scientific university is tentativeness, the student—very much alive—will seek life outside the academy. In the words of of two great Rolling Stones albums of the sixties: We want *Satisfaction* and *Now*.

If students sense a classroom message of tentativeness (distance, diffidence, delay: postponed life) they may well seek something now that is full, which is fun. The *academic* remedy for "diffidence" within the scientific spirit should be tenacity. Tenacity is to the scientific university what community was for the classical course. Tenacity is the determination to continue investigation, research, scholarship, and dialogue with the belief that this insistent inquiry will actually get somewhere. Tenacity creates an ongoing community that carries forward (maybe beyond this generation) the grand inquiry. Tenaciousness has its own achievements (quasi-classics). The modern curriculum may boast of uncertainty and inquiry-is-all, but one is tenacious in the quest because there are some honest-to-Something results. As previously claimed: The earth *is* more or less round.

Tentativeness and tolerance are all over the rhetoric of the modern university; it is the last "T" that is weakly expressed. Tentativeness and tolerance in a world of uncertainty are ready *life* virtues, good in the classroom and in "the real thing." Without, however, a tenacious belief in the process and progress of inquiry, tentativeness postpones life and tolerance is indifference. Put enough tolerance and tentativeness into the intellectual system and life's highs will have to be mindless.

I say that tenacity is not well articulated. This is not quite accurate. The tenacity that builds communities of inquiry, that creates "classics" (albeit a slight bit tentative), is certainly implicit in the enterprise of natural science, which is responsible for the new academic culture. It is the humanities (our modern "moral" liberal arts) that have failed to create a tenacious structure to replace the complacent community of the classics. No one will argue well for the classical list with just this humanistic material, but the real failure is that no one really *argues* about the value of any list, classical or trendy.

There have been strenuous attacks on the white male European bias of the traditional list of humanistic greats. An interesting observation and true enough. However, noting pedigree is not enough to assess value in either horseflesh or horse sense. Pedigree attracts our attention but it advances no arguments. The *argument* could be advanced either wholesale (pedigree is ideology, the social or biological determination of knowledge) or retail (these are the specific important values left out of the "canon"). Wholesale or retail arguments would engage real values.

Denominationalism had its dogmas; the humanities (and the modern university) need dialogue. Tenacious dialogue over the values embedded in the curriculum is the "moral liberal arts" equivalent of the institution of science: the ongoing commitment to research and testing that is the strength of natural science. Values are all over the modern curriculum, from the precision of mathematics to the passion of poetry (or from the passion for order in mathematics to the precision of language in a sonnet), but the values are like so many nuggets and nuts in a Christmas pudding. Of course the student may chew his or her way through the course catalogue, but leaving the digestion of values solely to the student's experience makes dialogue as mysterious to him or her as ordinary peristalsis.

Without a curricularly expressed structure of dialogue, it is no wonder that undergraduates and Allan Bloom believe that the university is a supermarket of higgledy-piggledy values among which the individual consumer may choose at will. That makes spiritual choice terribly easy and utterly boring. Supermarket spiritual shopping yields impulse buying. Values are not argued for because they are difficult and complex; they are instantaneous in whatever high is currently in fashion. ("Phi Beta Kappa" stands for *philosophia biou kubernetes*, "philosophy the guide of life"; a modern PBK would read "*pharmacia*" for "*philosophia*.")

The modern scientific university seemingly abhors indoctrination, even on agreed moral goals like the abolition of racism. There are no *university* dogmas to preach or denominations to defend. The claim sounds free and exhilarating, but as frequently interpreted by both its masters and apprentices (faculty and students), it offers a barren prospect for life and in the long run destroys the very institution it would defend. Dogmatically said: The modern scientific university needs doctrine and indoctrination as much as its denominational ancestor. In fact, because truth is so elusive and often distant (easy revelation being currently unavailable except by prescription) indoctrination in the *university way of life* is even more important than of yore. Unless students are convinced of the intrinsic value of the grand inquiry of the modern university, they will seek value in the extrinsics of career or in the various forms of human fun that have always prospered without academic facilities.

The old denominations spent endless hours rallying students to the way of life expressed in church and college. Modern universities spend a few moments of high rhetorical fancy, at freshman convocation and senior commencement, extolling the university. During the four years in between, the student will hardly avoid deep discussion, in the curriculum, of the structure, history, accomplishments, failures, aspirations of every human artifact *except* the university. Governments are analyzed, class structures dissected, science assayed, and families critiqued, but one will search the curriculum, required or elective, in vain for any serious discussion of the assumed values of the university itself. One might charitably conclude that academics think that simply being there will infuse academic value into students. A touching faith, like dropping aborigines into the Louvre (or art historians into the outback) and expecting that they would, of course, easily understand what was going on. I fear that the evidence is overwhelming— from fraternities to football rallies to funlessness to the lack of physics Ph.D.'s—that students don't quite get the point of the university. It is a nice place to visit, but one wouldn't want to live there. And in fact one doesn't *live* in the classroom at all; life is somewhere else.

The first section of this book has discussed "Mythos," meaning "story." My conclusion is that the university (the modern "scientific" university) fails to tell its mythos. Telling human stories is the function of the humanities in the subject-matter configuration of the modern academy. I regard this book as a sketchy attempt at constructing the university mythos—and if I offer any single remedy for the failure in life, fun, value, and study in the modern university, it would be to incorporate the self-conscious telling of the University Story.

When it comes to "full and fun," my own view is that the new universities won't replace old churches; as previously stated, universities are splendid at lots of things but make lousy religions. Nevertheless, the university has not been left bereft of spirit by tiptoeing out of the church of its founding. The university dissipates its life value, however, if it becomes only a supermarket of disciplines. The answer is certainly not a return to available dogma and fundamentalist indoctrination in any Testament, Old or New, classic, classy, or classless. The answer must be ongoing inquiry—and specifically a radically more self-conscious inquiry about the university itself.

I have said that the ontological lapse of the modern university is in the humanities. The story of the university is a story for the humanities. If the university itself—the choice of disciplines, the relation of science and humanities, the social function of learning, the pedagogies of subjects, the populations served—is not a subject worthy of examination in the university, it is small wonder that observers inside and out will conclude that there isn't all that much of value in university life itself. The university will be accepted only for its extrinsic value in producing economic analyses or scientific breakthroughs—converting the *life* of liberal arts (good in themselves) to mechanical arts (tools for some trade). Academics love the Platonic injunction that the "unexamined life is not worth living"; if so, the modern university's lack of self-conscious, structured examination *of* the university might well suggest to the unwary that the academic life is not worth living. Not only is the unexamined life not worth living, it is also no *fun*.

PART 2

Facts

This section's title is not entirely accurate. The great philosopher Santayana once said, "All history is myth corrected by further myth." In the sense that one story is superseded by a better, he is probably correct. In the first section I have sketched out the base story of the modern university: the mythos of the scientific research university. Although that story may *seem* to apply only to the megaplaces with their arsenals of accelerators and archives of ancient texts, I will risk disillusioning avid college-catalogue readers by asserting that the spirit of the modern university is everywhere extant. Old Cozy College is a (false) myth of the movies and admissions posters. Yes, the ivy is there, but beware: The faculty all graduated from Cal Tech.

The fact that the central engine of higher ed is research and scholarship, not piety and good morals, does not mean that teaching has died. Even Cal faculty can be friendly. The second section of this book deals with some of the secondary facts of life about modern colleges and universities. It begins with guidebooks—the first introduction, for many, to the future alma mater—and ends with an "afterword" about alumni. In between, there are discussions of some of the more puzzling aspects of everyday life in Academia Land. The first section tried to parse "liberal arts"; the second section discusses such mysterious issues as "What is the difference between a college and a university? Between a private college and a public university?" I discuss the mystification of prestige in college selection and some unmysterious items like sex. Fraternities, football, food, and how to fund a college education get some commentary. There is a chapter on "minorities" since educating diverse racial and ethnic groups constitutes a major unresolved problem on most campuses.

If the first section was the big myth, the second offers some lesser ones. There are facts, just facts, but I am loyal to the lesson of Mr. Metzger, that superb exponent of bull. The *meaning* of the facts is what counts.

10

Guidebooks:
Underground
and Over-the-Ground

I have been interviewed *twice* by Lisa Birnbach. She was in the final reaches of *Lisa Birnbach's College Book*, her preppy guide to colleges, and I was in the final stages of moving from being president of Bucknell to president of the University of Rochester. Within a month I had the opportunity to fudge about two distinguished American institutions of higher education.

It is quite impossible to tell the truth, the whole truth, and nothing but the truth about any college worth anything—particularly if you are the president. Any president who's been doing more than reading his or her own press agentry knows all sorts of things about his institution that he would just as soon not tell Lisa Birnbach. This bureaucratic reticence gives vogue to the "insider" guides that "tell it all" and "like it is." (Telling it "as it is" would indicate that the teller had a college education.)

A friend once described a college president as someone who goes around with "a permanent look of pleased surprise." Indeed. After years of the most careful cultivation and solicitation one receives a major donation to the building fund: It is always received with pleased surprise. This permanently pleased aspect of the president makes the guidebook author wary. He or she knows that this is not Ideal Institute. (Some exception seems to be made for the alma maters of the authors of the books. Lisa Birnbach thought Brown was terrif.) The guidebook author knows that the president knows the liver spots; why doesn't this personage 'fess up? The reason is not simple mendacity.

As a philosopher I teach existentialism in my spare time. One of my favorite quotations is Jean-Paul Sartre's definition of human being: "Human being is what is not, and is not what it is." Amen. And one could say the same about "college being." I like the saying not only because I think it is true but because it is puzzling enough to engage a long debate in class. Fortunately, it can be translated into more prosaic English. I will do so, but I insist that the paradoxical cast of the original is important. There is an element of bad faith, of lying, in telling the "inside truth" about a valuable being, human or collegiate. Thus, beware the presidential platitude and the guidebook attitude.

The prosaic translation of Sartre might be stated as follows: Humans are a combination of what they are and what they want to be. Put in Sartre's fancy terms, humans are a combination of "facticity" ("facts" will do) and "transcendence" (ideals). The same for colleges: They are facticity + transcendence. The problem with the formula for humans and institutions is the plus sign. Humans and universities are not a combination but a sort of inner contradiction of the fact and ideal. The ideal, if it is worth much, is always a critic of the facts. "What hand, what heart, et cetera, ever aced it?"

As for transcendence, only the church might pretend to more—and in that holy realm there is a penitential rite. The university, as the temple of rationality, intelligence, truth, art, and the full, fun life, is eminently available for the devastation of facticity. Combine that with the sense that faculty are underpaid and students are overcharged, and one has a ripe field for academic novels and insider guidebooks. They are the functional equivalent of confession—except that there seems to be no one (the *New York Times*?) to give absolution.

It is important, therefore, to understand the idea of an insider's guide. An insider's guide is always onto facticity and against transcendence. An insider's guide wants to show in what way the ideal is not met. An insider's guide to St. Francis of Assisi would want to show him kicking at dogs and pocketing the collection box. It won't do to show that really, down deep, he is a saint.

Insider guides are generally factual enough. Of course there are some that invent facts, producing the guidebook equivalent of the *National Enquirer*, but that is rare in my experience. The most noted insider guides (Fiske, Birnbach, *Yale Daily*) have made a reasonable effort to discover some genuine facts about the institutions evaluated. What is impossible for the insider guide is to convey the basic contradiction of every institution. The better the place the greater the contradiction.

The level of griping at the very best universities and colleges is extraordinary. I recall a visit to Amherst College. The faculty were most upset with the level of salaries. As a close administrative watcher of comparative salaries I was astounded; faculty salaries at Amherst then (and now) are among the very best in the country. It turned out that the source of the discomfort was a well-remembered saying by some former trustee in boisterous days before: "Amherst faculty salaries should be second to none." Faculty are both perceptive and (when necessary) literal minded. They had glanced around in Massachusetts and found a couple of places, at least, where faculty salaries were higher.

Any really worthy institution will have some of the "second-to-none" mentality. When I was at Princeton, one of my favorite lines from faculty complainers was "If this is supposed to be such a great university, why isn't it better?" I would not want to say that you can gauge the quality of an institution by the level of griping, but there is something in that theorem. Proper tension between aspiration and attainment is the engine of creativity. Given the necessary tension of the collegiate enterprise it is easy enough to write an exposé guide to any college—the worthier and the easier and the more desired the exposé.

There is an obvious desire to read exposé accounts of the rich and famous, since most of us are neither. Such personages and institutions of power and privilege are a threat to our own sense of assurance. Thus, it is consoling to read that the prime minister has a mistress or that the curriculum at Harvard is a shambles. This urge to level works well with the glitz of life, but it can be utilized as a strategy to avoid the genuine press of the True, the Good, and the Beautiful (in any order). The best colleges and universities, in their wayward and human-all-too-human ways, are dedicated to a long list (but not the whole list) of the worthiest of human achievements. Nothing could be more of a relief in assessing the worth of such challenging places than to analyze the food service.

If insider (underground) guidebooks are into facts and against transcendence, the outsider (over-the-ground) books are the facts and nothing but the facts. *Barrons, Cass and Birnbaum, Lovejoy,* and the like, are essentially catalogue compendia with demographic dressing. They are helpful for a quick comparison of the basic statistics: size, SAT scores, fraternities and sororities, list of available majors, and so on. The over-the-ground guides are as faithful as their compilers are diligent. They are not without error, however.

It is worth mentioning one of the more egregious and well-distributed sins of over-the-ground statistics. SAT scores are taken as a sign of excellence. However misguided the assumption that high SAT equals high rank, the fact is that they are so regarded by many and elegantly distorted by a number of colleges. The simplest distortion is to argue that there is a "normative" group of students at Upsurge U. and that the "others" (alumni children, faculty kids, football players) will "distort" the genuine paradigm at Upsurge. In the light of "honesty," the distorters are dropped and lo! the SAT riseth. This practice has become so widespread that the class of others has been labeled NIPS, which is not an ethnic slur but an acronym for Not in the Profile Statistics. Beware the nefarious NIPS.

If one goes beyond registrar's statistics (with or without alumni children) to "facts" about the quality of faculty and food service, the source and character of the facts need to be considered. Among the three evaluative guides the methodology for collecting information differs. The *Yale Daily* relies on student informants on the various campuses; Lisa Birnbach actually visited the various campuses and talked to all sorts of folks (including presidents); Ted Fiske and his staff have an elaborate system of gathering data from "student leaders" and "representative students" (not by any means the same group), faculty, and administrators. Each of these methodologies has possibilities in the midst of its problems.

The *Yale Daily* informants tend, in my experience, to be other newspaper types across the campuses. I am a great believer in the concept of student newspapers, though I am usually a skeptical reader of the daily product. Student newspapers are a necessary component of a campus and we would all be worse off without them. On the other hand, like their senior partners in the national news media, they are not into good news. Unfortunately, compared to the municipal police blotter, colleges are relatively dull and most of the really interesting things are good news. What student newspaper ever headlined a singular discovery by a faculty member or the fact that sophomore student Smith finally understood "Endymion"! The normal worries of any collection of humanity on the globe occupy most of the newspaper's concern: Housing, food, misbehaviors, political machination, and the cost of living predominate. Put those together with the insider's commitment to revelation and one has a sure prescription for a compilation of complaint.

A colleague of mine at Dartmouth became so exasperated with the student newspaper that he had buttons made in the type font of the *Daily Dartmouth* that read: "I have been misquoted." I don't believe that student newspapers "misquote" as much as "misplace" the news. What the *Yale Daily* hears over the telephone from the editor of the *Winsockie Whistle-blower* is probably an accurate account of some set of facts and opinions but it is not clear where it fits in the puzzle of collegiate fact and ideal.

If there are problems with the student informant, there is also the problem of compiling any conglomeration of opinion while remaining in the offices in New Haven. Lisa Birnbach had the good sense to imitate parents and applicants by visiting most of the 256 campuses on which she reported. Ms. B., having just come off writing the highly successful *Preppy Handbook*, had a very definite editorial focus in her campus perambulations. Chic and sleaze seemed to be her special interests, so that one wondered at times whether the evaluations were aimed more at subscribers to *Cosmopolitan* or *Penthouse* than the average high-school-age applicant. Despite the rather surprising slumming at some distinguished citadels of learning, Birnbach has a sharp reportorial eye for some of the social ambience at colleges. You won't get a sense of the psychology department, but at least the whole book has passed through the single evaluative psyche of Ms. Preppy herself.

Fiske's *Selective Guide to Colleges* originally appeared as *The New York Times Selective Guide to Colleges*, but the notion that the national newspaper would put an imprimatur on any assessment of colleges was so troublesome that the original title was scuttled. Fiske rates institutions rather as Michelin does restaurants. The loss of a star can cause suicide among chefs. The same urge no doubt strikes directors of admissions who lose a mortarboard on the academic ranking. Fiske's data collection is certainly superior to that of the other evaluative guides, since he gathers a wide selection of opinion from various sources. On the whole, his descriptions of institutions with which I am familiar strike me as recognizable.

The major problem of the Fiske descriptions is that they are, by the nature of his legitimate enterprise, adverse to advertisement. If one could simply believe the admissions-office advertisements, then one would hardly need Fiske, Birnbach, et al. to evaluate all those high-minded claims. To take a stand against the advertisement has a basic justification, but it is also misleading. In my Sartrean mood I will claim that colleges are also their advertisements. The prospectus sets out the beliefs that determine the guilt complex of the community. When Cozy College says that it offers close student-faculty relations and then discovers that nary a soul has showed up at the student-faculty social hour, the dean frets. The president of Prestige agonizes over his miserable department of xylophon-ophery.

The most valuable and accurate character descriptions of colleges would understand and assess the degree of failure and achievement, pride of accomplishment, sense of aspiration unachieved, fact, and ideal. I suppose there are those insti-tutions that fail by complacency—but I have never seen one. A much more common failure is a loser syndrome that settles over the whole culture. Such a syndrome is peculiar to really worthy institutions because they have reason for the loftiness of aspiration. They were once great; or there is one great school or department that causes agony to the others; or they sit on a hill overlooking Neighboring Most Selective U. Attending Downer College could be a dreary event.

I have commented on the adequacy of informants and eval-uators; let me conclude this chapter with some comments about one of the more widely noted evaluations, the *U.S. News & World Report* poll of the "best" colleges and universities. This poll would seem to have an ideal set of informants: university and college presidents. Who should know more about the character and quality of the industry than the presidents? At the risk of utterly disillusioning the reader of this book, I would respectfully assert that they are not all that worthwhile as eval-uators. Consider the nature of the top-ten lists. It does not take three hundred college presidents to tell the public that Harvard and Stanford are very great institutions; thirty subway conduc-tors would know that. It *would* be interesting to discover the most interesting colleges *not* noted by subway conductors. On that score, college presidents are only slightly brighter than the average. Most of us have led a relatively sheltered academic existence. The president of an excellent Midwestern college like Lawrence will have only the shadowiest notion about what is going on at Occidental in Los Angeles, and vice versa. We meet other presidents at various semieducational events, and one might guess at the quality of the institution from the traveling leader—but I wouldn't recommend it.

While I was president at Bucknell, the university was voted the "top comprehensive university" in the eastern part of the United States. We were all pleased, though I was not sure then (nor am I now) what a "comprehensive" university is. Nevertheless, from the little I knew about the rest of the colleges on the list, it seemed that Bucknell was probably the "best" of whatever that bunch was supposed to be.

Recently *U.S. News* published a survey of the hundred best U.S. colleges. The selection is systematically misleading, since the hundred winners are selected from such different strata in the educational establishment. They compiled the list by taking national research universities plus liberal-arts colleges plus regional comprehensive colleges plus community colleges plus . . . This is like getting a list of the hundred best baseball players by taking ten from the National League, ten from the American League, ten from the International League, ten from the Little League, ten from the Oconomowoc Mechanics and Gas Station Attendants Hardball League and Marching Society, and so on. On any Sunday afternoon in April all these characters may be the best on the local diamond, but as a whole the list is not a collection of all-stars. Many of the very best institutions in the country simply won't appear on such a listing. Last year, Oral Roberts University made the cut but neither of my favorite places (Bucknell, University of Rochester) did. With all due respect to Brother Oral and all those good folks in Tulsa: With or without my administrative skills, Bucknell and Rochester are clearly superior. Perhaps I should starve myself in the Library Tower until *U.S. News* confesses its error. (I note happily that in the current edition Rochester made the top twenty-five national universities without my having to practice ascetic denial.)

As several of the evaluative guidebooks say, their best function is raising in the minds of students and parents colleges not otherwise considered. I agree, and would like to write a book that never mentioned Harvard. (This is not it.) Choice of college is so wildly underinformed that institutions considered generally come from only two sources: local connection (hometown college, alumni alma mater) or the "hot" places—institutions so well known that they may be named for dramatic effect on a TV sitcom. (It means something, presumably, if a character is identified as a Berkeley student, but one seldom hears about Davis, Riverside, or Santa Barbara. Or, as the Irishman said to the pastor: How come you talk so much about St. Paul and never mention Minneapolis?)

11

Universities by Any Other Name

There are a number of educational institutions about which I fully expect to remain in a state of invincible ignorance. A particular instance is Burger King University in Florida. I mention this higher hamburger educational emporium because it illustrates one of the great puzzles to the layman: What do you have to do to be called a "university"? If the class to be defined includes Berkeley, Burger King, and Bologna—the city in Italy, not the sausage—I despair of offering any assistance.

Even without taking Burger King into consideration, academic nomenclature regarding "universities" is mostly mishmash. The University of Rochester has been a "university" by name since its founding in 1850—when it surely wasn't anything like a university even in the Burger King sense (*in sensu rege burgeriense*). "University" may have noted the vaunting ambition of the founders, but it applied to almost nothing in reality except the sign over the rented quarters in the United States Hotel. At best, Rochester at founding was an exceedingly modest college with a couple of faculty members and a classical curriculum of Greek and Latin. There are still "colleges" styled "universities" that have as much or as little right to the title as Rochester did at the beginning.

On the other hand, there are "colleges" that in terms of the quality of the faculty, the range of research, and the existence of graduate programs would certainly count as "universities" if they had a mind to it. Dartmouth College is the prime example. Dartmouth is a powerful academic institution, which years ago gave its name to one of the landmark Supreme Court cases. (The Dartmouth College Case, argued for the College by alumnus Daniel Webster and with majority opinion by Justice John Marshall, establishes the law of private corporations.) Once having won a landmark case, an institution is not likely to chuck its name even for greater academic glitter.

On the whole, one can make a fairly sharp distinction between colleges and universities on the basis of graduate programs. Institutions with graduate programs and/or professional schools are certainly universities, no matter how they choose to call themselves. Institutions that staunchly and proudly serve only undergraduates are certainly colleges.

But it is not that simple.

Bucknell is a predominantly undergraduate institution with no doctoral programs and only a handful of masters' degrees. Nevertheless, it calls itself a university. In this instance there is piety to founders—as in the case of Rochester—but also a justification in the breadth of the offerings. Unlike the typical liberal arts college, Bucknell has an engineering school and a sizable program in management studies—an area not traditionally covered by a liberal-arts institution. So, since this is a free and generous country, one may grant Bucknell the title university. Middlebury College, on the other hand, chooses to remain "College" despite the fact that it probably has more graduate students than undergraduates and offers a very large number of masters' degrees and a small number of doctorates. (The secret of this anomaly is the Middlebury College Summer School [of foreign languages and English], which is predominantly at the master's level.)

The confusion of nomenclature is a product of the complexity of institutions, advertising advantage, and even state legislation. For many years football fans about the nation were delighted to receive the scores of the Bloomsburg–Slippery Rock game each fall. These two institutions seemed to the great public to be the quintessential unknown rural schools of the nation; few could have said what they taught or even where they were. Even alumni of these two schools may have had difficulty placing them on the educational map. For many years Bloomsburg, Slippery Rock, Lock Haven, and others of similar charming designation were "normal schools," that is, teacher's colleges, which prepared students to teach in the public schools. Following World War II many of the old normal schools were converted (and upgraded) to "colleges" not only in Pennsylvania (the location of Slippery Rock) but in DeKalb (Illinois), Eau Claire (Wisconsin) and so on.

Titular enhancement has continued apace. In the last ten years Slippery Rock has moved beyond "College" to "University" by courtesy of the legislature of the Commonwealth of Pennsylvania. Presumably the legislators in Harrisburg envied their cousins to the north who had created the SUNY system (the State Universities of New York). The SUNY system was constructed by taking former normal schools (Oneonta, Geneseo, and so on) and designating them "State University of New York at . . ." SUNY also captured some distinguished private institutions (Buffalo) and created some ambitious "university centers" (Stony Brook), but that is a more complex story. The Pennsylvania elevation is somewhat more misleading than the New York terminology, because instead of creating a SUP System (State Universities of Pennsylvania at . . .) the legislature called the former normal schools–cum–colleges "universities" straightaway. So, overnight, Pennsylvania had a host of "universities." The sudden advent of a Bloomsburg University in turn caused a scramble in the private-college domain. I personally was involved in the upgrade of good old La Salle College into La Salle University, in part as a response to the competitive pressure of the new state designations.

It might seem from this scramble for university title that "university" was clearly the preferred name. It might also seem that the whole matter of designation is merely a public-relations invention to attract notice in the market. Not quite so. It is clear that many institutions are very keen to retain the designation "college," since they believe that it most clearly spells out their main mission as undergraduate institutions. Some real universities with blossoming graduate programs may envy the title "college" because of its inherent attraction to undergraduates who fear that they will be ignored, slighted, and abused in the intense atmosphere of a "research university." Because of the attraction of the "college" title some major universities go to great pains to create a separate college for undergraduates. Thus, undergrads at Yale University are in Yale College, and the University of Chicago, by population predominantly a graduate and professional school, has "the College," which has even had separate faculty appointments.

The "university" designation, vague and vaporous as it must seem, is also not merely a public-relations fiction. Excepting those institutions that have carried the title "university" historically despite their exclusively undergraduate programs, institutions cannot in most instances blithely change the sign over the academic portal. The State of Pennsylvania undertook a rigorous investigation of La Salle before permitting a change in the charter title. It was necessary to describe the graduate and professional programs, library resources, faculty capability, and so forth before the visiting team of accreditors would permit the change. The consumer has every right to expect that a place called "university" is something more than a liberal-arts college. The problem will be to find out what is the "more" that the title encompasses.

Let us assume that you are dealing with a "real" university, that is, not with Siwash U., which was so named by its grandiose first president in honor of the equally grandiose donor Hezekiah Siwash. It is simple enough to see whether you have a real university at hand by noting first of all the extent of graduate degrees offered (including professional-school degrees). The more degrees offered the more universityish is the institution.

There are several great universities in the country which

were originally founded solely as graduate and professional schools: Johns Hopkins, the University of Chicago, Clark University in Worcester, Massachusetts. It is interesting to note how each of these institutions has dealt with the issue of undergraduate education. In all three cases, economics more or less compelled the creation of undergraduate programs. The undergraduate college is usually the best "customer" base for the enterprise, since undergraduates pay tuition fees while graduate students are often carried wholly on scholarships. Hopkins started an undergraduate program, while Chicago created a separate "college." Clark, on the other hand, has evolved from an exclusively graduate institution into a predominantly undergraduate college with a few distinguished graduate programs retained. (The evolution of Clark began with the founding of the University of Chicago, which aggressively raided the Clark faculty. William Rainey Harper was not called a "captain of erudition" for nothing!)

In between the true research university, with its range of Ph.D. and other doctoral programs, and the exclusively bachelor's-degree college are those institutions that are "universities" because they comprise multiple schools (even if these are dominantly undergraduate) or because they offer some range of master's degrees. On the whole these "universities" are in temper and spirit more like colleges than they are like the Ph.D. universities of the land. A student or parent who chooses the non–Ph.D. university because of its university status is likely to choose it because of some special program, such as engineering. The "more" that one receives from the non-Ph.D. institution is a horizontal "more," not a vertical one.

Universities *are* different—even if they carefully construct or cocoon in their midst a "college" for undergraduate use only. In the first place, most universities are just downright bigger. The University of Minnesota is a great state university with some 35,000-plus students. (When I lived in Vermont it always fascinated me to realize that many universities in the country had more citizens than did Burlington, the largest city in the state.) Universities do more in more subjects at more levels to more people than colleges do. Simple as that. There are modest-sized universities, however, that approximate the size of the larger "colleges." Princeton has some 4,500 undergrads, Rochester about the same, while Columbia, Rice, and Chicago have undergraduate colleges with under three thousand students.

More important than the population is the range of facilities that have to be in place for Ph.D. work. The fields most obviously demanding in this way are science, engineering, and all technical areas. If an institution offers advanced work in such subjects it simply has to keep up with the state of the art, so that students are much likelier to have access to the most advanced instrumentation at a university than at any except the most affluent or specialized of undergraduate colleges. While it is not as obvious, the "facilities" for nonscience specialties are also more expansive at the university. There is a formula used by accreditors, to the effect that library holdings in, say, history must be ten times larger for a Ph.D. program than for the minimal B.A. program. Finally, of course, there are faculty at the university who are more extensively and more densely networked into their fields and allied professions than is likely to be the norm at a collegiate institution.

In sum, universities, like supermarkets, offer more. But there is the complication. There are folks who prefer a friendly corner grocer to a grandiose line of overstocked shelves. At least this is the rhetorical thrust of the colleges toward their (pretentious?) university colleagues. Institutions that proclaim college status suggest with some reasonable basis that because they are *exclusively* devoted to undergraduate education, students do not have to vie with Ph.D. types for lab space or chase after an absent research-faculty member who is so busy ringing his network that he has no time for freshmen.

As a faculty member at both major universities and liberal-arts colleges, and as a president, at different times, of each kind of institution, I am not about to wound either my present or past employers by settling this presumed quarrel between collegiate and university types. There is a basic truth to the claim of the collegiate institutions. If there are nothing but undergraduates to instruct there is nothing to distract attention from undergraduates. There is certainly an ethos, arising from the proclaimed belief in undergraduate teaching, that can create a rather different atmosphere at the undergraduate college. However, the contrast can also be seriously overdone. University faculty are more or less human beings just like college faculty. The men and women at university centers conduct classes with young people in a manner not noticeably different than the day-to-day conduct of college faculties. The proverbial visitor from Mars dropped onto a set of campuses to observe the daily teaching tasks in History 101 and French 12 would have a very hard time keeping track of when the class was in a college setting and when it was at a university.

It is also a considerable exaggeration to suggest that college faculty think only about their undergraduate charges while university faculty are absent for research. At the very strongest colleges, faculty carry on a very active research life, which may or may not have a direct relevance to their normal classroom activity. Swarthmore College has a more generous leave policy for faculty research than many universities. "Publish or perish" is not exclusively a university vice—if it is a vice at all.

A more telling distinction is between the "distinguished" university or liberal-arts institutions and what, for lack of a general term, I would call service colleges. At these "service colleges" faculty are *exclusively* involved in undergraduate *teaching*. The normal contact-hour (i.e., classroom) courseload with students is at least twice that at a research university and at least a third greater than at the leading liberal-arts colleges. The faculties at these institutions essentially do not pursue research and scholarship; there is scant institutional support for or expectation of such work, and they would have precious few moments for research after correcting all those papers. University faculty often cast aspersions on such teaching arrangements. It is often said that the relation between research and teaching is like the relation between sin and confession:

If you haven't done the one you have nothing to say at the other.

There is no question that faculty at exclusively teaching colleges face a very difficult task even "keeping up with the field," not to mention contributing research. Just how important "keeping up with the field" may be to the average student is the point of contention. Elementary calculus probably hasn't changed much since Leibniz, and Latin is a dead enough language that one doesn't have to read the latest best-sellers. A good bit of the introductory work will not necessarily profit from a Nobelist at the rostrum. My own personal experience with faculty at exclusively teaching institutions is that they are remarkably dedicated and surprisingly knowledgeable given the demands put on them by their teaching commitments. Such faculties can be genuinely challenging to students, if only through their own combination of dedication and frustration. Nothing would please them better than to have one of *their* students go to Stanford for graduate work. The University of Scranton is not by anyone's lights a national name, but it has had a remarkable record in producing Fulbright awards for students.

The most important distinction is not college-versus-university as such; it is the academic expectation of the institution. There is more in common between the top liberal-arts college (say, Amherst) and the small research university (say, Princeton) than strikes the PR office. Once an academic quality level is set, the expectations of students and faculty at top colleges and universities are much the same on a daily basis. The research university of quality just has to have more extensive libraries and laboratories. Finally, of course, the university has no noticeable *top*. For the advancing and ambitious, it is possible to go right on through the undergraduate curriculum into the most advanced research and extensive scholarship.

In addition to being dean of dropouts at Princeton, I was given as an antidote some custodial care of the University

Scholars program. This program attracted the very, very most talented students, and they were essentially given free rein across the course offerings of the university. Since *visible* extra-high talent in adolescence tends to be mathematical (not metaphysical) most of these students were in math or a natural science and most were doing graduate courses by the sophomore year. That is a capacity which the research university alone can offer.

12

Service and Saga

Private higher education is a unique American phenomenon. University College Buckingham is the only possible contender for that title in the United Kingdom, and it has had great difficulty getting proper governmental recognition. Alan Bond, the Australian entrepreneur, has put $200 million (Australian) into the establishment of the first private university Down Under. One will search in vain across Europe, Asia, and Africa for the likes of America's private institutions. There is a reason.

Private higher education was one of the ways in which Americans solved the religious problems that convulsed Europe after the Reformation. Instead of state religion and state education, the Americans were to invent the right of conscience and private schools. The oldest of our colleges were predominantly denominational. Even into the nineteenth century, various denominations rushed to establish their own Baptist or Methodist or Lutheran seats of higher learning in the local area. The connection between religious sponsorship and private incorporation was constitutionalized by the First Amendment in the Bill of Rights. Separation of Church and State—the somewhat misleading construction of the explicit wording of the First Amendment—has been a vexing and complex issue for the courts as they examined the place of denominational schools and colleges in our national life. Despite rulings that permit some state assistance to denominational schools, religious schools remain decidedly "private."

However, they have not necessarily stayed *religious*. Princeton may have been founded as a strict Presbyterian college, but that fact probably escaped Brooke Shields during her recent sojourn at that venerable seat of learning. The vast majority of the pre-twentieth-century colleges and universities of the nation were fiercely denominational at their origins. The vast majority of *that* vast majority are now nondenominational, pandenominational, or "secular" depending on one's preferred description.

The "private" *and* "secular" college turns out to be a peculiar historical artifact. One can understand the need for private *religious* colleges but what real difference is there between Stanford (private) and Berkeley (public) other than a stiff tuition fee? It is worth attempting to characterize the difference, which proves to be subtle—to some it will seem insubstantial—yet, I believe, it remains significant.

In some very important dimensions there is almost no difference whatsoever between private and public institutions *of similar character*. "Similar character" is the important qualification. At the blackboard it is probably impossible to distinguish an educational difference between a major state university and a large, private research university. Cornell may be something of a proof text, since it is basically a distinguished private university with a sizable "public university" component in its college of agriculture. To the best of my knowledge the public-sector agronomists and the private-sector economists exist happily side by side without any sense of spiritual schism.

When one makes comparisons of public and private institutions of "similar character," one almost always chooses to compare major research universities because it is that kind of institution which appears most similar across the public–private line. With a few exceptions (for example, New College, a former private institution incorporated into the Florida system), there just are no *public* liberal-arts colleges. Thus, the student aimed at a liberal-arts college is already set on a private direction.

Between the research-university similarity and the liberal-arts dissimilarity are a set of qualitative and programmatic differences that are not as easy to delineate. For instance, there are very few *small* major research universities—and none that are public. Cal Tech is as glossy a research institution as one could hope to find; it has fewer than two thousand (highly selected) undergraduates; it is private. Princeton, Chicago, Washington University in St. Louis, Johns Hopkins, and Rochester have small student bodies by comparison with any of their quality peers in the public sector.

Conversely, there are no real equivalents in the private sector to the state colleges–cum–state universities that have blossomed from normal schools (or been created) since the end of World War II. These new or blossomed institutions offer broad programs of traditional studies and practical training on a geographically accessible basis. Most are relatively large and are—by choice and facts of life—not highly selective.

The growth of the public-sector colleges–cum–universities has encroached on the traditional clientele of some of the older private colleges, particularly those which offer any sizable "practical" curriculum (undergraduate majors in business, nursing, and so on). A number of Catholic colleges were originally much like the new state colleges, in serving a geographically determined clientele with a mixed program of practical and liberal-arts study. St. Xavier in Chicago, founded by the Sisters of Mercy, has for obvious reasons provided nursing training for Catholic women in the area. The existence of state colleges with a service orientation in the Chicago area encroaches upon, in part, the traditional mission of Xavier, De Paul, Loyola, Rosary, and the other smaller Catholic institutions of the diocese.

All opinion surveys indicate that the general public makes

a distinction between public and private on the ground that "private" indicates "higher quality." To those of us who work in the private sector of higher education, this is some consolation when considering the financial stress of private schooling. However, it is not a very accurate characterization. There certainly are differences between public and private, but a general view that "public" means "lower quality" will hardly serve. I do believe that the University of Pennsylvania ("Penn": a private institution despite the name) and the University of Texas at Austin (a fabulously well-endowed public university) are *different*—but I do not believe it is academic quality that is at issue. The very best of public and private are excellent without qualification. I am equally certain that some state colleges are the feeble creatures of local political enthusiasm, as some private colleges are the relics of religious passion wholly spent. Quality is not their issue either.

Is there any *character* difference between private and public that is worth consideration? I continue to believe that there is a distinction.

The sociologist Burton Clark made a study several years ago of what he called "distinctive colleges." A distinctive college was one that had a "saga." He cited such institutions as Swarthmore, Antioch, and Reed. All of these are liberal-arts colleges and all are private. It is not surprising that a "saga" can be most easily detected on a smaller scale, but I would argue that it is the presence—however attenuated—of "saga" that distinguishes the private institution from its public brethren.

Clark characterized the saga as a story that enclosed the academic progress of the student—as well as faculty and staff. In going to an institution with a saga one enters an already existing dramatic story line that clearly identifies the style of education as distinctively "Swarthmore" or "Antioch." In contrast to the distinctive institution with its strong story line was the "service" institution, where one accumulated credits and eventually got enough points for a degree. In the service institution one uses the college to get a skill and a credential; in the distinctive institution the saga "uses" the student and faculty

to continue its strong story line. At the service institution one
emerges with a degree in psychology, at the distinctive institution one emerges as "a Bryn Mawr graduate."

In general, our public universities and colleges are institutions of service. That was their charter at origin; that is the
great function they continue to fulfill. Even our most distinguished public universities continue to act as service institutions to the citizens of their states. One will acquire a very
distinguished degree in physics from Berkeley, but one does
not expect to enter into a "Berkeley saga." (Except, of course,
that Berkeley students have invented a sort of extracurricular
political saga, which continues more or less to the present day.)
For all that they may be alike in quality, Stanford has a story
line that Berkeley need not and probably cannot quite emulate.

An institutional "saga" may be extremely self-conscious or
marvelously understated, but in the great private institutions
the educational story line *is* the institution. Sagas may come
in curricular content, in pedagogical form, or in what, for lack
of a better term, one would have to label life-style. St. John's
College in Annapolis is a pure case of a "content" saga. St.
Johnnies engage in a four-year compulsory curriculum, which
entails reading the "Great Books" starting with the Greeks,
then the Romans, and on into the modern world, with senior
year devoted to the twentieth century. Swarthmore, in contrast,
offers a curriculum that in content is standard for liberal-arts
colleges (except of course for the secret of the Swarthmore
engineering program). The saga at Swarthmore is pedagogical
form. The great reforming president of Swarthmore, Frank
Aydelotte, introduced the "honors" program to what was at
the time an unremarkable small college with strong football
and fraternities. In the honors program some Swarthmore students do no formal coursework in their upperclass years. They
prepare themselves for comprehensive examinations in their
honors subject. You can be a classics major at Swarthmore
just as you can at Pomona, but you do it differently.

Content or form creates a special style for students at these
colleges. A common four-year content with the same instruc-

tors across the curriculum creates a density of argument and discussion that is as distinctive as it is unique. Advanced study that climaxes in an outside examiner's review of achievement produces a certain self-reliance and audacity that mark a Swarthmore honors graduate.

There are other ingredients that create the complexity of culture and style at these institutions. Swarthmore would not be the same without its Quaker sensibility, and St. John's retains the moral fervor for world peace of its Great Books Founder, Stringfellow Barr.

Not all private institutions have such self-conscious sagas as these two very interesting liberal-arts colleges. One might wonder whether the large private universities have any distinguishable story. It is hard to say that Harvard, Princeton, or Yale has a very distinctive content to its curriculum, and the pedagogical form is hardly peculiar. One is tempted, however, to suggest that the Iviest Ivies have a powerful "saga of style." The saga of these institutions is partly a result of sheer longevity. The layering of history at the great historical universities always suggests a saga—even if one is not quite sure what it is. Surely an institution with a statue of Nathan Hale in front of his old dormitory, or a university formerly headed by Woodrow Wilson, or the alma mater of Franklin Roosevelt must have *some* tale to tell. It may be only a saga of "importance"—but a sense of importance is important.

To a certain extent the association of saga with private institutions is almost always a historical hangover. There have been few private colleges and universities founded in this century—founding is too expensive. Private generally means "historic," and the sense of some history at hand cannot be duplicated by the most generous modern state subvention. Most private institutions, because they were born of denominational fervor, certainly had a definite life saga to preach and promote. They did so with a will. Although denominationalism has largely vanished from the academic grove along with the elms, its ghost lingers on in the determination to have some message that informs life and study.

The distinction drawn between public and private may seem illusory. There has been a great deal of interesting imitation between sectors. The University of California at Santa Cruz was established to create the Golden State equivalent of the Yale College/Harvard House system (small residential and academic sub-units). It was an attempt to create liberal-arts-college substructures within a large state university. New York University, which is as large as any decent state institution, advertises itself as "a private university in the public service," thus taking on some of the service mantle normally associated with public education.

If all else fails in distinguishing public and private education, it is worth concluding with a clear-cut and unfailing distinction: modes of governance and control. As a private university president I speak to this issue with conviction. To the average student in Chem 102, the way his or her university is governed probably makes no difference whatsoever, and the odds are excellent that during a four-year curriculum said student will never really detect a difference. Nevertheless, I believe that there is a vital difference between an institution that is essentially self-governing and one that finally has to answer to the state board of education or whatever political governing body may be in place. There is an immediacy to the private-university community that is impossible to achieve when the local authority has to clear decisions with Albany, Harrisburg, Springfield, or Sacramento.

It is not accidental that state-university faculties have unionized while those of private institutions have not. There is a legal bar to private-college unionization, on the ground that faculty are not "labor," they are "management." That judgment by the Supreme Court seems to me to fit the facts. At a "mature" private institution—to use the court's language—faculty are in a strong position to determine the course and character of the institution. At public institutions faculty's position is less clear. Faculty have considerable "managerial" power at mature public universities; the fact that state institutions are unionized often stems from specific legislation that permits the unionization of public employees. Nevertheless, a deeper truth is expressed by the unionization of state faculties. Because of the necessary layering of authority within any state system, faculties simply do not have the immediacy of control that exists in the private institution.

My final conclusion is that public universities remain the great service-providers of higher education in the country. Many are extraordinarily effective and count as national treasures in which the citizens of their respective states should take great pride—even if the football team doesn't get a bowl bid. Private institutions, on the other hand, because of history, saga, and governance, provide a special sense of continuity and community that public education finds hard to replicate.

13
Minor Matter of Majors

In the first section I attempted to locate the Snark-like liberal arts. One of the images of "liberal education" was general-purpose education, as contrasted to specific career, technical, or professional education. For students facing the collegiate curriculum, however, there is a puzzle about the notion of general (nonspecialized) education. The major puzzle is the major. If the basic lesson of liberal arts is "generality," why do students then have to choose a major specialty?

The ideology of the undergraduate course of studies rests gingerly on the educational topology of "breadth" and "depth." There are two basic curricular facts of life at most colleges: the breadth requirement and the depth requirement. Because of the fundamental allegiance of the American system of higher education to the "jack of all trades" school of pedagogy, "core curricula," "general education programs," "distribution requirements," and the like are virtually universal. Even determinedly preprofessional programs insist on some distribution pattern outside the pre-profession and its allied subjects. These breadth requirements are the first hurdle faced by most students. To the eager freshman itching to "get on with it," core requirements may appear to be underclass academic hazing. Art majors just *have* to do calculus because everyone needs "formal skills." If lack of interest weren't bad enough, the aspiring Mary Cassatt only scored 325 on the math SAT. Small wonder that "distribution requirements" are something that students feel has to be "got out of the way" before the real education begins.

Because of the formidability of breadth requirements in the minds of most students, I want to say a few good words about the whole notion. Breadth requirements vary. Some colleges have a totally required four-year curriculum (rare but very interesting), a few places are utterly freewheeling and self-consciously have no requirements at all, at all. (A curriculum that has had a considerable vogue with students but is looked on with some degree of disdain by faculties at more "traditional" institutions.)

There are two basic methods of curricular construction for the breadth requirement. Harvard's postwar history illustrates both types. For many years Harvard had a series of carefully constructed, specially staffed general-education courses, which covered major areas of knowledge and practice that "everybody ought to know." There were courses on natural science, social science, the arts, and so on. Within the past ten years this older curriculum was "reformed" into what are generally called "distribution requirements," in which various already existing courses are designated as exemplifying the basic concepts of natural science, social science, the arts, and so on. Let me name the two Harvard modes "general education" and "distribution requirements." The essential distinction rests on whether the breadth requirement is met by specially constructed courses or by having already existing courses designated as distribution fulfillers. (The distinction will do but is not perfect: Many an existing course will be retooled if the distribution label falls upon it. Nevertheless, there is a tendency in distribution schemes to leave the character of the course largely in the hands of the department in which it is offered.)

Given that most schools require the breadth component, which system is preferable: general education or distribution? There is no clear principle of choice. General education is a heavier-duty requirement (because there are specific courses); distribution gives a considerable choice across a range of possibilities. (Critics of the Harvard distribution scheme claim that its range of choice is wide enough to remove any philosophical point from the requirements.) Generally speaking, general education indicates a higher level of collective institutional commitment than distribution requirements do. The collective commitment is gen ed's virtue and vice. Given the independent-mindedness of students and faculty, the trend is definitely toward individual choice in roughly circumscribed areas (distributions) rather than the consensus of the gen ed programs.

Some of my Harvard friends claim that one of the reasons that the older gen ed program died was that the generation of its teachers reached retirement. One advances in academic life on the back of specialties, not general education. Teaching physics to poets is not the straight path to a Nobel Prize.

(A historical footnote: The great schemes of general education in America have a rough relation to times of national peril. The Columbia gen ed program was a post–World War I invention, as the so-called Harvard "Red Book" general education stemmed from World War II. It was argued that if the nation was asking its youth to fight in order to make the world safe for democracy, the least universities could do would be to let the troops know what democracy was all about. Defenders of Western civilization needed to appreciate what they were defending. Absent a war and absent much apparent agreement about what is civilized in Western civilization or whether it should be Western at all, the construction of collective curricular consciousness is notably difficult. Distributing civilization across individual departments and faculty seems more politically plausible.)

Professorial critics often regard distribution requirements as catalogue pieties and/or rationing faculty resources. Can anyone really believe that one year of required college science gives deep insight into the subject? The alumni body of every college is littered with survivors of required French who cannot utter a *"merci."* Distribution courses are a means of forcing students to spread around the faculty so that not everybody is in Econ 101 at the same time. It gives the out-of-fashion areas something to do and helps them snag the occasional major.

A certain measure of controlled skepticism about breadth requirements should not obscure two general truths about the genre. First, the faculty members who teach these courses are often deeply dedicated to the concept of distribution and to their specific topic. While there are smug institutions that assign the required courses to the most junior faculty because they are a burden and a bother, the majority of institutions, in my experience, are deeply concerned to display their best wares in their biggest (often required) courses. Thus, the chance of getting good teaching in required distribution courses is better than average. Second, however raggle-taggle the philosophy, construction, integration, and execution of breadth requirements, they are a fixed fixture in American higher education. Wayward as they may be, they do respond to the democratic urge for commonality of educational experience and to the notion that Americans will display broad and general skills in profession and career. A spate of required curricular wandering is a better template for actual life than the determined careerist curriculum.

The standard distribution package rests on a shadowy philosophy of "areas of knowledge" usually tied to skills necessary for life, career, and further study. The most common areas track the usual divisions of the academic disciplines: humanities, natural science, social science. Foreign language is a frequent addition, returning of late from the limbo of the sixties, probably as a reflection of the inroads of international business into the economy. Students are required to take two courses in each of the designated distribution areas. The program as executed may have one or two high hurdles (often a math, or foreign-language requirement), but most programs have some softer landing spots for the unskilled and unenthused. "Rocks" and "stars" (geology and astronomy) seem to be the favored gentle roads through natural science.

My conclusion on distribution is that it does little harm and some good, and is here for the distance. Basically, distribution responds to the continuing sense that higher education in America has to be general and cannot be strictly professional (in the European way). Distribution remains as a lingering piety that American colleges are unlikely to reject but that— given the disciplinary demands of modern professorial commitment—is unlikely to command great enthusiasm.

If faculty enthusiasm for breadth is limited, commitment to the major is real and intense. For all the allegiance to the liberal arts and to general education, American colleges and universities almost universally insist that students *major*. This is one of the crucial decisions facing students either at admission or during the college career. (At most institutions the final date for deciding a major is in the second year.) The major is regarded as the key to work, career, and profession. No one asks the pre-med or the chemical engineer what he or she intends to do. That seems obvious. The philosophy major will be queried incessantly about what the major is good for.

Next to the choice of college—and often as an ingredient in that choice—the choice of major is most important. It is much easier for a college adviser to recommend a specific college if the student already has a clear-cut sense of a major. If you want to major in optics (which is not lens grinding but the study of lasers and all sorts of light) you come to Rochester or the University of Arizona, since they have the only undergraduate programs in the field. That is an easy recommendation. Choosing a school when you want to major in English is not so easy.

The standard guidebooks can be helpful and sometimes accurate in specifying which departments at which places are the best. What guidebooks don't do is give any sense of why one might choose this or that major. Everyone, including the writer of college-catalogue prose, seems to assume that, like Liberals and Tories, students are simply born into their major convictions. In the spirit of the age, one might label this the sin of "majorism." At least, it is true that the confused applicant or hapless freshman who cannot claim a major on the instant is likely to feel distinctly second-class.

I applaud the curricular importance of the major, and three huzzahs for those entering students with long-range vision on profession and career. (My eldest had such visions since age thirteen, my middle daughter changes visions every year.) Statistics show, however, that the average student changes majors three times in a college career. Its importance is matched only by the inscrutability of many of the choices and strange silence from the learned about the deep values of their subject areas.

President Derek Bok of Harvard, despairing of the advising system—a common enough failing at all colleges, as far as I can ascertain—decided that all Harvard students could read, and so he had published a most useful little book entitled *Majoring at Harvard College.* In the booklet are succinct and perceptive essays from the various departmental chairs about the inner intellectual virtues and outer vocational interests of the various disciplines. Every college should have a similar publication. In a book of modest size—and as an author of modest academic range—I cannot hope to unveil the inner joys of everything from archaeology to zoology, so I will limp out of this section by arguing for the importance of the major in the course of general education.

I justify the general-education value of the major via commentary on one of the purported disabilities of the current crop of college students—and (alas) some graduates: poor writing skills.

Since the source of this complaint is often middle-aged faculty and middle-level managers (who hire the graduates), it is worth wondering whether the current younger generation really does write worse than my generation (of the fifties). Perhaps we were just as inarticulate but have somehow learned language in the postdiploma years without actually noticing it. There is some evidence that writing really has deteriorated. I offer an intriguing piece of research.

It is obviously difficult to compare student writing across generations. How do you get samples of vintage fifties sophomore essays? Simple. A writing researcher at Michigan facing this problem repaired directly to the fraternities, which have been keeping files of papers written since the 1850s. Because faculty possess certain habits it was even possible to find the very same *assignment* from thirty years ago. Was there a difference? Yes, but the nature of the difference proves most interesting. It turned out that on close reading the students of the fifties and of the eighties hardly differed on such stylistic matters as spelling, punctuation, and sentence structure. Where they diverged markedly was in the inability of current students to sustain an argument of any length. One could blame this on a writing style developed from thirty-second commercials and bumper stickers, but the fact of the matter seemed to be that the main deficiency was bringing together facts, opinions, and ideas in a connected fashion. I have tested this finding with my Rochester faculty colleagues and they tend to agree with the Michigan findings.

The connection to a major is clear. A major is nothing but a *large* connected argument. Students who do not major are deprived of the experience of one large, long, complex, sustained argument; the mind knows only bits and pieces. Even a patchwork quilt has an overall design. (I point out that there are a few colleges where there are no majors but where the entire curriculum becomes one large and interconnected argument. The important thing is a large connection, not subject-matter specificity.) If there is a problem with the major in American colleges it is often that the large *connection* of the argument is not well drawn out in the course of study. Some of the standard "majors" are sufficiently compendious that one may wander aimlessly about in and through various sectors without ever having a sense of what history or psychology are as large arguments.

In the long run having a major in the undergraduate years

is probably more important than the major's content. Of course students should go toward career interests if they are clearly perceived, but an undergraduate major in musicology may serve the future senior manager well. (The former chairman of my board of trustees attended the university's Eastman School of Music, presumably without the foresight to see that he would be president of the USAir Group.) Life's most important skill may well be argument—not contentious wrangling but the ability to take all the jetsam of the day and make it cohere in a large, perspicuous connection. This is the inner life of any major.

Finally, of course, one needs to major in the Metzger method of bull. Cowing through a major may get one into grad school but it won't win the Nobel in the field and will be useless in municipal-bond trading. The virtue of the major is not its content but its form. Metzger didn't know much about anthropology, but he knew about making a long connected argument with premises, examples, conclusions, digressions, conjectures, and speculations. I have often used as a teaching method what I call the Map of Madagascar Ploy. One asks the student to draw a map of Madagascar. Most folks can't spell "Madagascar" let alone draw it. They object. Unfair? Not at all. We all know enough about maps to raise questions of form. Where is the capital? Is it on the coast? Is there a coast? Near the mountains? What mountains? Drawing a free-form map of Madagascar raises all the right questions, for which the actual facts will supply the right content. Knowing a major is knowing the form of connected discourse; with verve you can draw a map for everything from management to marriage.

14

Some Like It Hot

There is the tale (unverified) of the Princeton-grad parent who moved heaven and earth to get his son admitted. The admissions office politely refused, counseling the father that Jimmy just wouldn't make it in a tough academic environment. It would be a negative and defeating experience and the young man should seek another fine institution where he could succeed and enjoy his college experience. The father insisted, and finally said that he didn't care whether the young man flunked out on the first day of school. It was the case in those days (and may still be) that once an individual is *matriculated* at Princeton he is a member of that class forever—regardless of academic success. Junior would be forever a member of the Princeton class of '62 regardless of the fact that he failed to successfully complete a single course. The admissions office was intrigued, but refused admission.

For this parent, the outcome of higher education was not important, it was the in-come. (The pun probably has some relevance.) Various studies of higher-education choices have noted that (at least after flowers) "prestige" is the most important factor in college choice. Prestige is an associative virtue which comes from the name of the institution. It need not say anything about the actual education of the graduate. Of course, the odds are relatively good that a graduate of Old Prestigious has some specific strengths, if for no other reason than that prestige begets selectivity, which begets strong students, which begets prestige.

A companion tale to the eager-father story is of a verifiable set of articles in the *Daily Princetonian*, on Princeton admissions policy. The articles detailed various grumbles from faculty about the quality of the students, and suggested that someone should shape up the admissions office. A student wrote a very interesting counter. He argued that obsession with admissions policy suggested that there was precious little that the curriculum and faculty could do to improve intellectual function, so it was vitally important that the students be bright before they arrived. This was a version of Harvard President Abbot Lawrence Lowell's sour remark that the reason universities are such great repositories of knowledge is that the freshmen bring some in and the seniors take none away, so knowledge accumulates.

"Does it make a difference which college one attends?" The answer depends on whether in-comes or outcomes are at issue in the choice. If one is interested in outcomes then I would argue that one can get a very decent education at all sorts of highway and byway places in American education. On the other hand, if in-come—not graduation but matriculation— is the important matter, then one is rigidly restricted to the current pop list of prestige places. Word of mouth will be more valuable than rationality or guidebooks, because prestige is a word-of-mouth affair. Only when the name falls trippingly from the tongue in the proper boardroom does prestige exist in the flesh.

One may think that the list of prestige places, while short, has some range as well as geographic and social spread. This is doubtful. Aside from Harvard, Yale, Princeton, Stanford,

MIT, and . . . well, let me see, it is remarkable how unknown even old, well-established, excellent colleges can be. Try saying "Colby" in Los Angeles or "Mills" in Chicago. The prevalence of "hot" colleges among the young and their elders is a function of the highly mysterious character of actual educational excellence. One is sure that there have to be more really good colleges than HYP and a few friends—and of course there are. But factual markers are generally lacking, so lunchroom rumor can create a hot property on fleeting reports.

Students themselves are often extraordinarily uncertain about the prestige rating of an institution, even when it's their own. My oldest daughter attended Mount Holyoke, clearly an institution of venerable tradition and academic excellence. It took her two years to realize that she did not have to answer the question "What college are you going to?" by carefully saying "Mount Holyoke?" with a rising inflection. (Like "I live in Hickville, I am *sure* you never heard of it.")

If a student or parent has his or her heart set on attending a college that will bring instant recognition and nods of approval from distinguished elders and jealous peers, then one simply must consult the pop charts. Unfortunately, we do not have a Top Forty or a best-seller list for prestige institutions. A rough approximation could be made by looking at the headlines about higher education in the *New York Times*. It is important that you only read the *headlines*. You want to know whether the *name* of the college is sufficiently important to catch the interest of the headline writer. Once you get into the body of a story, the name of the institution is bound to arise, so that will not do. There are certain names that regularly make the *Times* headlines, while there are clearly other universities that, though covered in some detail, fail to rise to the top of the bottle.

My favorite example of the importance of headlines comes from a casual meeting with the president of Brown University. He was fulminating at the *Times*. He brandished a large front-page headline that read, "FORMER HARVARD DEAN SAYS . . ." As a matter of fact, this former Harvard dean had been a member of the Brown faculty for five years. However, Harvard hit the headlines; Brown—at least in this instance—did not.

A parenthetical thought: Of course if all one wants is some sort of name recognition, then one should go for the area of widest name recognition: athletics. It is always possible to have the average man know *something* about your university if it has just won the Rose Bowl. One has to be cautious with athletic prestige. Notre Dame is probably the most noted athletic name in American higher education. While the fathers of the Holy Cross are properly proud of the university's athletic heritage, they are even more pleased with the fact that in the last twenty-five years, Notre Dame has come to be recognized for its academic excellence.

I have already indicated that the distinction between "rational" and "romantic" factors in college choice is not the clearest ever. Lack of female or male companionship could certainly count as rational consideration in an individual's life plan. Since prestige is an in-come–related issue, it could also count as a rational motivator in seeking admission to a particular college. In the parlance of this book, however, the *rational* choice is related to outcomes and to the educational experience available at a particular college or university.

There is a reasonable correlation between "hot" and "good." I can't think offhand of a hot college where one will not get a good or better-than-average education. I can be reasonably certain of that judgment, because "hot" propagates "good." Most faculties can teach up to whatever clientele is before them, so that as "hot" attracts more students, the admissions office is more selective, the eye of the average undergrad is brighter, and academics are better. If the quality of the student body were the only consideration in education, "hot" would be an infallible guide to "best." Unfortunately for this direct theorem, faculty need to be factored into the equation.

While it may be an empirical fact that "hot" generally implies "good," the converse is by no means the case: Non-"hot" does not imply non-good. More important, some non-"hot" higher education is (I do firmly believe) superior to some of the more overheated choices of the day. The sources of heat in colleges and universities fall within my principal divisions of rational and romantic. There are hot colleges that are just so because of all the most rational outcome reasons one could imagine. MIT is as hot as a cool engineering school should be, and on rational grounds: faculty, facility, funds, and the student body attracted by all that. On the other hand, there are institutions currently on the hot list which, while they are certainly worthy, have attained their current temperature by happy accident.

Sometimes "hotness" is simple temperature. Hot schools tend to be clustered in sun (preferably with oceans) or snow (preferably with mountains) and not in between. Surfing or skiing help raise institutional heat, if not prestige. Colleges of the plains, such as Grinnell, Carleton, Knox, and Beloit, have a hard time hitting the hot register except among cognoscenti who appreciate a dedicated academic tradition. Exciting cities are a lure. Boston has become Youth City, U.S.A., and every Boston institution of higher learning profits from the fact. (Also, given "hot" Harvard, which certainly rates rationally, any Boston student can be a Harvard student manqué by just hanging out in Cambridge.) The attraction of Youth City also helps explain the lure of some of the largest state universities, which are self-made cities of the young. Given enough people of the right age in Minneapolis or Miami Beach, someone is bound to create rock groups or organize games of shuffleboard, as the customs of age may dictate. Large universities become a focal point for appurtenances of the culture of the young. NYU regards the location of Tower Records' main store in their immediate location as a distinct admissions lure. Finally, hot schools may well attract celebrity students. Brown University has had a succession of sons and daughters of the rich and famous in recent years. There must be a deep (if unsubstantiated) belief that famous people know something about colleges that is unrevealed to the average literate applicant.

More interesting than the adventitious charms that may beget heat in schools is a consideration of what seems to block a connection between achieved excellence and applicant attraction. Since "hot" and "prestige" imply that one has a name-brand school, the matter of name is not incidental. Princeton is fortunate in "Princeton"—it hath a noble ring. When visitors tour Nassau Hall at Princeton, they are likely to be shown a large and imposing portrait of a colonial governor of New Jersey. It seems that this worthy donated some trifling sum to the College of New Jersey, located in the hamlet of Princeton. In gratitude for the gift the curators of the college offered to name the institution in his honor. He declined, and so the school became known by the place name. Since the governor's name was Belcher, one must judge that he did the Ivy League a favor. It just wouldn't be the same with Harvard, Yale, and Belcher leading the way.

Noble name itself may not suffice for perceived nobility. Washington University in St. Louis has had a most distinguished academic record, but there are at least fifteen other "Washingtons" across the nation with which it can be confused, as well as with—worst of all, perhaps—D.C. and government itself. Confusion between public and private institutions is no help in establishing heat. As noted earlier, private education is generally regarded as better according to public-opinion polls. The University of Washington in Seattle is an excellent public university, but it is no help to (private) Washington University in St. Louis to be confused with its West Coast almost-namesake.

The title "University of Place Name" is universally associated with public education. The University of Rochester, although a well-endowed private university with a long history, is widely regarded as a branch of the State University of New York. A graduate applying for a position at the Chase Manhattan Bank in New York (a moderately sophisticated operation) was unable to discover Rochester in the list of institutions on an employee application until she spotted something called SUNY Rochester. In a poll of applicants to Rochester, we discovered that 41 percent believed that the school they were applying to was a public institution. (Of those who said that they knew the university "very well" it was 27 percent!) When I suggested that this was a problem for the university I was told that "University of . . ." was not a fatal misdirector. Consider the University of Chicago: Everybody knows that Chicago is a private university. In our poll, over 50 percent of the students thought Chicago was public.

There isn't much one can do with a name—at least after history has wended its way. The University of Pennsylvania has managed to change its name by adapting its nickname in all its publicity. It is simple "Penn" now and I note that their admissions picture has brightened considerably. (What could we do with "Roch"?)

While there is no infallible linkage, I believe that there is a certain rough connection between higher rationality and lower temperature; at least, it seems to be the case that higher rationality has a hard time overcoming lower romance in public perception. My suspicion on this topic rests on the curious coolness of the American public to institutions of the most splendid rationality. The University of Chicago is an institution that has enjoyed the deepest "rationality" since its founding. Because Chicago came late in the history of higher education it could not trade on tradition for recognition. From the first, then, Chicago has taken more thought about education overall than almost any other higher-educational institution of which I am aware. The founding president, William Rainey Harper, had the most elaborate and impressive plans for education in a blossoming twentieth century. Chancellor Hutchins was an enfant terrible among college leaders. Many would question the wisdom of his educational vision—but at least he had one, which he was determined to preach on all occasions. To this day, Chicago maintains an enviable seriousness about its educational enterprise; but the school is not a hot property for undergraduates. To a certain extent the coolness of the clientele is based on an accurate perception: Every college claims to challenge students; Chicago really does. Maybe average applicants would like something "lite."

Serious institutions may have serious image problems in a romantic world. I was bemused to see a picture of President Hannah Grey of Chicago throwing a Frisbee (or was it a football?) on the Midway recently—no doubt to add a dollop of frolic to the image of the City Gray (the nickname of the University of Chicago based on the color of the buildings, not the current president). I wish her luck.

Single-sex colleges—I believe they are all women's colleges these days—suffer from similar seriousness. To attend a single-sex college seems to signal *Akademisch über alles*. That attitude isn't cool, so women's colleges are seldom hot. To avoid a truly great school like Bryn Mawr for second-tier Coed College lacks rationality.

A final category of the nonhot worth consideration: The most neglected distinguished institutions in America as a class may well be the great reform universities, that is, the universities founded on the European assumptions of the new era in American education. Because they were the creatures of the new age, these institutions carry less of the history, heritage, tradition, and "romance" of the older classical and denominational colleges. Nevertheless, they are in many ways the purest expression of the new curriculum and the new professorate that came to dominate all of higher education. Chicago is one of these, and I have already noted its singular strength. There are others. Cornell has seldom received the same enthusiasm as the older Ivies because it was a reform university, founded in 1865. Johns Hopkins was the quintessential European reform university at its founding. The University of Rochester came to prominence when Jacob Flexner caused George Eastman to found the first new modern scientific medical school in America. The rest of the university followed that model.

Lacking the charm of colonial portraits and the razzmatazz of collegiate traditions, the reform universities with their fundamental rational assumptions seem less romantic to the applicant, as admission statistics from most of the institutions would indicate. They are, however, a "best buy" for the serious student. The quality of the faculties and facilities is in most cases world class. The paradox and promise of these institutions were expressed (poignantly) by a dean at one, who said: "We would never lose a faculty member to two-thirds of the institutions to which we lose applicants."

15

The Effable

Despite all the guidebooks, newspaper exposés, and alumni newsletters, the quality of colleges remains a mystery in an enigma in a shroud and so forth. Evidence shows the dominance of flowers and Fluties as factors of decision and understanding. While both are fascinating, it is not clear that they have any direct relation to the quality of a college or university. If applicants and their parents are in fact intrigued by the horticulture, the fault is by no means theirs. It is extremely difficult to assay the essential factors that determine collegiate quality.

There are two reasons for the opaque character of college quality. First, within certain very broad ranges there will be no readily perceptible difference in overall institutional quality. As with breakfast cereals and Nobelists, it may be possible to rank order the range, but one is never sure to what purpose. Corn flakes may be better than shredded wheat and Einstein better than Bohr, but so what? Of course, if one takes a range broad enough to include Stanford and Siwash, it is relatively easy to detect differences, but that is not the normal task.

The second reason that hierarchizing higher education is so difficult is that the markers of fine distinction are unclear, unpublicized, and ambiguous. No one will be wrong to think that a major private or public university is "better" as an institution than the spanking-new community college down the road. (Always understanding that Spanking New may be better for applicant Doe than Glossy State University Center would be.) But how does one make decisions among and between the Ivies, between the Ivies and the major state universities, the Ivies and the reform-university cadre, the reform universities and the leading liberal-arts colleges, the members of the Associated Colleges of the Midwest, the Claremont Colleges and so forth unto the last split hair? The choice is ineffable.

This chapter will do what it can, however, to eff. While this may seem precisely the futile exercise inveighed against in the third paragraph above, my intention is not so much to decide between Brown and Dartmouth or between Hopkins and Carnegie-Mellon, as it is to set up some checkpoints of character. While I believe it is extremely difficult to make a really *bad* choice of higher education in America, I have been dismayed to discover too many cases of applicants and families bypassing exceptional opportunity for lesser light but more heat.

It will come as no surprise to a reader of this book that the most important *rational* factor for choosing institutions is the faculty. The quality of an institution is directly commensurate with the quality of the faculty. As one of my colleagues at Rochester put it: A college can be no better than its faculty— but it can be worse. The whole statement is important. There are ways to assess the quality of a faculty and they will have a weight in determining the quality of the university or college. However, an institution may have a faculty distinguished by every known mark and yet fall below collective excellence.

I recall a conversation with a philosophical colleague at one of the leading university centers in the country. I asked him, "How is the department?" He recited the current staff, which was composed of some of the most notable names in the field. A strong faculty if there ever was one. He added, however:

"But there really isn't any department. X lives down the coast, Y is in the capital, Z is up north. They never meet as a department." For graduate students this faculty may have been perfect—since graduate education is often individual mentorship or sponsorship—but I would have my doubts about whether it was ideal for undergrads. I would prefer slightly less notability and mobility, combined with a collective interest in the teaching of metaphysics to the masses.

Putting aside for the moment the way in which the multiple excellences of faculty may fail to function fully, it is worth pointing out some of the eminently effable characteristics which can be discovered with persistence in appraising a college or university.

The Ford Foundation recently sponsored a conference to which it invited representatives of the fifty leading schools of education in the country. Ranking schools of education is a daunting problem, since they suffer from (in former Berkeley dean Bernard Gifford's phrase) "congenital prestige deprivation." If one made a leap of faith and accepted that these fifty were the top schools (of some twelve hundred) what did they have in common that made them excellent? The answer: They appointed only faculty who had been educated at leading schools of education, that is, from one another, that is, from the other fifty chosen by the wizards of Ford.

Silly or circular as it may seem, this is not a bad way to discover excellence, even if one is not sure what the inner essence of such excellence may be. (When Ford went further to see if there were any inherent, describable character of the schools which defined them, the only common factor was that the faculty attended a lot of conferences!)

In the general university case, nothing is more significant in determining the quality of a college or university than whether the faculty has been educated at quality colleges or universities. Both the undergraduate and graduate schools the faculty attended are important, with the graduate degree being more so. Most colleges publish in their catalogue a list of the faculty, along with the places from which they hold degrees.

A quick scan through that list will give a rough check of the quality of the faculty's education—a quality that they are presumably anxious to pass on to the incoming freshmen.

I assume that it is easy enough for the ordinary reader to recognize the recognized star institutions of higher education. Thus, a faculty with graduate degrees from the Ivies, the great Midwestern and Far Western state institutions, the reformed-university group, and so on, has been well processed. While it is far from an infallible guide, the American Association of Universities (AAU) constitutes (by its own internal choice) the fifty or so *leading* graduate and research universities in the United States and Canada. A faculty that has degrees largely from the AAU list is reasonably assured of being strongly educated.

A small warning sign could be too much localism in a faculty. Did half the faculty get its degrees from the local state university? Even too many degrees from Harvard can be a problem. Dartmouth moved up in academic brilliance when it stopped the practice of departmental chairs hopping the Boston and Maine for a weekend of recruiting in Cambridge. The very best colleges and universities recruit on a national and international scale. The list of faculty degrees in the catalogue will signal infallibly whether the college under contemplation exercises that scope.

After the easy task of noting the distinction and dispersal of diplomas, the next refinement on discovering faculty excellence is more difficult and problematic. One of the best evaluators is whether this faculty receives prizes, fellowships, grants, and awards from external sources. One can start by counting Nobel Prize–winners, but since they are all scientists (and, lately, economists) the list doesn't have much range. Besides, Nobelists often have such stature that they are far removed from undergraduate teaching. (Exception: Princeton, to which the King of Sweden recently paid a visit in recognition of the fact that the nine Nobelists on that faculty *all* teach undergraduate courses. Certainly a recommendation for Princeton.)

Nobelists are rare, so it is more feasible to search out whether members of the faculty under consideration have received Pulitzers, Guggenheims, National Science Foundation grants, National Endowment for the Arts or National Endowment for the Humanities awards, and so forth. An ambitious admissions office may have those facts at hand, but if not they can be searched out by reading the president's report for the past five years. (Almost every college or university publishes an annual report. It often contains much more interesting information about the institution than the admissions brochure does.) Besides the special prizes, there are various "academies" to which the leading faculty of the country are elected by their peers: the National Academy of Science, the National Academy of Engineering, the American Academy. One can also inquire as to the presence of academicians on the faculty.

Prizes and academies are not normally touted in admissions literature, because they are "insider" academic info. Since the average applicant may not be too clear about the difference between the National Academy of Science and the Motion Picture Academy of Arts and Sciences, the academic "Oscars" are simply not mentioned. There may be a subtler reason for their omission: These various recognitions generally come from standing in the discipline and standing in the discipline generally comes from (dread word) publication.

The standard drama, reenacted with liturgical precision on *n* percent of college and university campuses every spring, is the tragic demise of a dedicated teacher who failed to get tenure because he or she did not publish. It's "publish or perish," and those who perish are, it might seem, always those special, vibrant teachers who fail to conform to the dry rubric of academic advancement. The standard scenario has truthful instances. The tenure review process is far from infallible and it is true enough that some gifted teachers are shunted aside because of minimal publishing. But the standard scenario is also far from common. The publicized cases are seldom reported in the context of the whole class of reappointment decisions. Most "negative reappointments" do not present the compelling contrast of superlative teaching and nonexistent publication. When a negative decision is made there are usually problems all over the record.

At any good college a faculty member rejected for tenure (after the usual probationary six to seven years of appointment) is bound to be a teacher of some accomplishment, or else he or she would have been eased out at an earlier reappointment decision. In appraising an institution's commitment to teaching, I would put very little stock in a current controversial nonreappointment. As the saying goes, there is less there than meets the eye. Even more important than the mechanics of reappointment and tenure is the real relation between publication and teaching competence. There is obviously no *logical* relation between great teaching and multiple publication. There have been noted, great teachers who spurned publication—though, if the truth be told, they were cut more in the culture-conveying mold of the old classical curriculum. Conversely, it is easy enough to point to Professor Dryasdust whose work on early papyrology has won her or him the Légion d'honneur but who should only be assigned to teach mummies. Anecdotes, as noted earlier, do not make data.

But if there is no logical relation between publication and excellence as a faculty member overall, and a teacher in particular, there is a factual connection. The essence of publication is not sixteen articles with 123 footnotes per year, it is placing your scholarship before a larger (professional) public. At the Eastman School of Music, "publication" from the oboe faculty is performance. Since this faculty is teaching its students to perform, it would be distinctly odd if they themselves did not. Publication is drawing together one's skill and placing it before a public of peers; it goes beyond drawing one's skills together only for nonpeers (students). The analogy from the Eastman School has some general validity. The history teacher is not teaching the subject only for the inside of the student's head. Presumably one gets the lesson if one can "perform" as well as know in the heart. A publishing faculty sends a message of performance to the student body which may be more important than the date of the Battle of Lepanto (1571).

There is a price of course for a publishing/performing faculty. The Cleveland Quartet (the Eastman School resident string group) is on the road part of the year, so the number of students in their studio is necessarily limited. Your favorite physicist may be at the Tokyo accelerator. I would not for a moment wish to demean the utterly dedicated faculties at exclusively-teaching institutions who are not thus distracted, but if one must do some hierarchizing of educational energy I have to conclude that faculty who are active performers bring an excitement to the campus that the teaching-only institution cannot attain. So, I would check the college bookstore for the row of recent faculty publications.

If a researcher means to make a lifelong avocation out of collegiate appraisal, there is an interesting refinement on counting publications. In certain fields there is what is called "the citation index." These indexes are not interested in how much one publishes, but in how much the work is read. Thus, they count the number of times an author's work is cited in someone else's publication. Roughly speaking, the more citations the more famous the author. There are limitations on using the citation index. By that method Zeno (of the paradoxes) would be the most famous philosopher ever. Every subsequent philosopher cites Zeno to refute him. Perhaps the road to citation fame is to say something compellingly ridiculous.

In addition to recognitions for research, scholarship, and "public performance" various national teaching awards are also offered. The existence of such national award–winners on a campus is interesting but not overwhelming. The national teaching awards are relatively few, so that a large cadre of excellent teachers go unrecognized. An even less reliable teaching indicator is the faculty-to-student ratio. At some reaches of extremity—if there are very few/many faculty and very many/few students—it must say something. But within limits it is almost impossible to tell what the faculty–student ratio actually means. Some major institutions have "research faculty," who get counted as faculty but do nothing for teaching. An institution with a relatively large faculty is likely also to have a generous leave program. (Large faculty means more financial resources means more scholarly opportunities for faculty.) The effective faculty–student ratio—counting faculty on leave, students abroad, and so on, is extremely difficult to obtain. Many of the general guidebooks refuse to publish the statistic: There is no common system of counting, so whatever figure is printed is uninterpretable.

Having assessed as best one can the quality of the faculty, the next logical question is: How will the faculty and student body meet? There are two aspects to the meeting of faculty and students: physical and programmatic. One of the virtues of rural schools is that faculty are physically close to the campus. Amherst College has maintained an extensive program of housing for faculty near the campus to maximize physical proximity. If one has a geographically dispersed faculty, the mere physical meeting of faculty and students becomes a concern. While rurality fosters proximity, city universities may maintain a neighborhood, for example, the University of Chicago and Hyde Park.

Physical proximity has possibilities, but it is program that counts in the long run. The most important program is the curriculum. Even in the most *intime* of colleges, I would venture that 95 percent of the clocked faculty-student time is curricular, either in class or advising for classwork. The earlier discussion of the mythical M. Chips outlines the basic student-faculty proximity points of the modern college. In assessing the ineffable character of student-faculty interaction (assuming one has already hit on quality faculty) I would look to two clues. The first is most obvious. If you have selected a faculty of performance, do the students get a chance to perform with the faculty? It surely is *intime* when the Meliora Quartet (students) performs the Mendelssohn Octet with the Cleveland Quartet (faculty) at Alice Tully Hall. Is there a functional equivalent in the general curriculum? That is, can students do research alongside their faculty mentors?

The second curricular clue would be almost any special variant on the normal courses of accumulating credits. It may be an honors program (Swarthmore), a core curriculum (Chicago), freshman seminars, a luncheon program with faculty, a free day in the week for extracurricular artistic/intellectual/laundry events (Rochester's University Day): something that indicates a *self-conscious* effort to activate the student-faculty relation beyond the classroom. The fact of the matter is that the standard undergraduate course of study is so standard and so routine that it can occur on any campus as a by-product of the registrar's office. Any curricular experimentation—even unsuccessful experimentation—indicates that the institution is actively seeking to create a student-faculty conjunction.

The importance of faculty quality for making a proper judgment about quality of colleges cannot be overstated. One thesis of this book has been the rise of faculties, so they deserve prime consideration. There is the oft-told story of the occasion on which General Eisenhower was being introduced to Columbia University. The general, who had been appointed president of this great institution, met in the late afternoon with the faculty assembled. He expressed his pleasure at being able to meet "the employees of Columbia." A senior professor rose and said, "Respectfully, sir, we are not *employees* of Columbia University. We *are* Columbia University." And so it is.

A few miscellaneous items nevertheless. Students are hardly miscellaneous at a university. Despite the previous anecdote, a collection of scholars is not a *university* unless there are students to be taught. One can assess the quality of an institution, up to a point, by assessing the quality of the student body. SAT scores, rank in class, geographic diversity are all "objective" measures to be weighed—though beware the NIPS (Not in Profile Statistics) in the statistics.

The main problem with factoring in student data is that students are not all that *different*. American young people are the products of a homogenized national culture, which is further refined by the college selection process. I recall an exasperated admissions director at a highly selective college who was being criticized for the "homogeneous" character of the freshman class. "I should admit a few really dumb ones. That would be diversity." One is likely to find more or less the same sort of folks at all the colleges of one's choice. It is difficult, then, to discern real differences in student bodies. A really diverse set of student cultures on the short list might read: Brown, Wayne State, Oklahoma, Pepperdine, and St. Wapniacl of the Woods, and almost no one chooses over that range.

A final item to be considered as an "objective" correlate of quality is—one blushes to mention it—money. Money doth not guarantee quality education, and poverty can produce a determination for advancement that poshness cannot. Nevertheless, an institution with secure financial resources has a flexibility of response that is precluded to the more financially constrained. During an accreditation at Yale, I noted to the president that Department X was in a difficult state. He agreed and said that they had done "the usual Yale thing" when the problem arose. "The usual Yale thing" was to hire three nationally distinguished X-ologists. I asked whether it had worked. "No," he said. "It was still a lousy department, but with three distinguished faculty members." Well, that was some improvement.

With a source of funding, one can create new programs, purchase new hardware, attempt to correct old mistakes. Colleges and universities are on the whole highly constrained economically because they rest on people and programs that are locked in by everything from medieval precedent to modern tenure. Restructuring a university is like moving a graveyard. Change for the new or correction for the old comes largely from additional resources rather than reallocation. In a word: money. Thus, in the case of public institutions it is worth reading the newspaper to see whether the state department of ed is on a stringency diet. For private institutions, endowment resources and fundraising are generally correlated with quality. When all else fails to rank: Look at the size of the institutional budget divided by the total student body. You can believe the figure—in a skeptical sort of way.

16

Other F's

Having effed the essentials of academia, it is now safe to turn to the eminently nonacademic effables of colleges and universities. Happily, most of the effables are F's: football, fraternities, food, fun, footprint (the place of the place). These aspects of college are much easier to assess than the strength of the biology department. You can get the athletic win-loss record from the local press. Fraternity presences (and other social organizations) are well noted in catalogues and both food and fraternities are regularly reviewed by the various evaluative guides.

It would be pointless to question winning statistics. One might as well accept at face value the food and fraternity evaluations of the guidebooks. It is the student stomach that is the final arbiter. The food (etc.) gradient of a college is not trivial. Bucknell happened to have an excellent food service—so much so that we attempted to get the *New York Times* to send their restaurant editor on a tour of college cuisines. We were confident of a three-star rating. The food really was good, but the

secret of success was an utterly amiable *maître de cuisine,* who
bore the slings and arrows of student complaints with such
unfailing joviality that one could hardly fault the food forever.

All things being equal, the rational choice would be to attend
the college with Rose Bowl prospects, *cordon bleu* chefs, and
partying worthy of Sardanapalus. (One may have to attend a
classical curriculum to catch the reference. I do not know the
college epitome of partying for the present age. It used to be
Chico State—probably because unwary readers thought it was
named after the middle Marx brother! The president assures
me the label no longer applies. When he banned drinking on
campus, someone blew in his front door. But the school's
reputation has changed.) All the fun things should be located
in an ideal location for both symphonies and wind surfing.

One of the educational outcomes of college attendance is
discovering that life seldom optimizes all possibilities simultaneously. All things are not equal and choices have to be
made in the effable. In this chapter I want to suggest the plus
and minus of four principal *F*'s in order of ascending cultural
determination: footprint, food, football, and fraternities.

Footprint

Where a college is may be highly determinative. Skiing is not
good in Nebraska and symphonies are hard to come by in rural
settings. More strictly academic possibilities can also fall within
geographical lines. Urban studies courses are more likely in
an urban area. Most of the locally determined sport and scholarly choices are obvious and well detailed by the institutional
catalogue. What is not so clear is why colleges are where they
are in the first place. There is always a reason, and it may
speak to the nature of the institution even today.

The siting of colleges and universities runs the gamut of
rational possibilities: the founders wanted to provide local service, refuge and retreat, pay off a political debt, or boost the
area economy. A very rough approximation of the reasons for
location starts along the urban/rural division. Rural colleges

have generally been founded to escape the vices of the cities. To escape the vile influence of Harvard and Boston, Williams College was located in the remotest part of western Massachusetts. Repeatedly, spiritually inclined founders sought a place in the forest where young men would be safe from whatever was the then-fashionable moral infirmity. Some of that sense of refuge lingers on. The coming of the interstate highway system makes monastic moral insularity harder to come by, but "Escape from the rat race of . . ." remains a potent lure for rural colleges across the nation.

Urban universities (if they were founded when there was a city, rather than having a city descend on them out of the suburbs)—tend to have been founded to serve some special function or population. Right up to the 1950s, many Catholic universities were founded in cities because of the desire of church authorities to offer higher education to their flock. Secular city institutions were often created to meet the needs of lower-income students, of a business-oriented population, of government, and of the other larger works of the society that cluster in major urban centers.

This urban/rural split offers the major high-minded reasons for locating a college here rather than there. There are less lofty premises. Boosterism was one of the major spurs to college founding in the nineteenth century. Local real-estate interests discovered long ago that a neighborhood called University Heights or College Park lent a certain panache to commercial trade. (Alas, many of these nineteenth-century commercially created colleges went with the neighborhoods. The number of nineteenth-century colleges that have long passed out of existence is soberingly high.) State institutions' siting often resulted from a combination of boosterism and pork-barreling at the state capitol. This practice continues. The presence of a branch of the state university in some underdeveloped region may be the economic anchor for the area.

Whether the original motive was high or low, monastic or mendacious, colleges are inevitably where they are. Place will be ambiguous to any general slice of the admissions group. A colleague at Dartmouth—a decidedly rural institution whose founding notion combined missionary enthusiasm with monastic sobriety—reported on a survey regarding location. The results indicated that half of those surveyed came to Dartmouth *because* of its location, the other half *in spite of* it. A predecessor president at Rochester liked to argue that it was the perfect place for a serious university: The weather guaranteed that study would proceed without distraction. (Ireland is not the island of saints and scholars for nothing: Consider the weather.) My guess is that students divide along the Dartmouth line: They come because and in spite of the location and the climate.

There are fads and fashions about location. At the time of this writing urban universities are back in favor after a period of disdain. Cities appear to be "where the action is," and there are some institutions (unnamed here) that enjoy buoyant admissions profiles less because of their academic credentials than their immediate access to a tram line.

In the long run it is worth remembering that the prime-time location of *all* colleges is the library (or the lab or practice room). Higher education, in the last analysis, goes on in the restrictive space between the head and the book. Dumas once defined theater as "one square yard and a passion." Given the proper passion, any academic yard will do.

Food

In discussing this text with my college daughters I was complaining about the food ratings given to colleges by the various guidebooks. Who goes to college for the cookery? I was assured that I was quite wrong. They agreed that university food is not great food but dining-room distress will generalize itself across the curriculum.

The problem of university food is universal. One of my former colleagues used to give a speech to the freshman class praising the quality of the food services, which were indeed exemplary. He would conclude, however, that even at its best university cooking is institutional cooking, and it will not be as good as Mother makes. He urged the students to write home and tell Mother just that.

College food services are provided either by an internal staff or an outside contractor. Both have possibilities. An internal operation with high institutional pride is the surest bet. There is a deep local investment in the dining arrangements; the boss of the works is available and responsive. Next best is a college kitchen that has just hired an outside commercial firm. Inevitably they send in their best available crew, and the quality of the food is noticeably improved. The worst of all possibilities is a local, entrenched food service that the central administration cannot figure out how to demolish.

Food ratings for the college of your consideration should be taken with a grain of salt. Administrators really are (despite my daughters' doubts) apprehensive and responsive on food issues. Reports on the quality of dining are not restrained—and it is a dim administration that does not act on bad service or bad food. On the unrestrained character of the consumer: I recall eating dinner at home one evening when a great knock came on the door. At the door were two students who had traveled some four miles out in the country to my house with a plate of food from the college dining hall. They said that as dean of the college I should see what stuff they had to eat. I gazed at the offered plate with some discomfort; it looked like the famed "mystery meat" that is available exclusively in college dining halls throughout the nation. As good luck would have it my six-year-old was standing by. Not being too anxious to reprise my own college dining memories—they were generally awful—I invited Elizabeth to try some. "Say, that's pretty good!" she said. The students were somewhat deflated, but I can only assume it was the sheer novelty of the dish that appealed.

College dining service is in my experience pretty good, as far as it goes—even four miles out of town. Whether food affects the curriculum or vice versa, it is one of those facts of life around which the myths of satisfaction or its opposite can be spun. I end with my favorite myth. My undergraduate food memories are almost all bad. The setting of the meal could not have been more impressive: the small, oak-paneled, Gothic-windowed dining halls of the Yale College system. These halls had been designed by planners who envisaged candlelight and napery. It was, however, the postwar era and twice the planned-for number were being accommodated. We did not even have *dishes*. Sitting under arched ceilings eating off navy-surplus tin trays removed the last vestige of charm from a dubious cuisine.

Except for the strawberry endowment. Every spring from the very caves that produced nondescript potatoes would emerge the most opulent strawberry shortcakes, with fresh biscuits and mounds of whipped cream. The story was that some rich Yalie had left a strawberry endowment for the purpose of propping up the laggard scholars in the spring.

As I have so much else reported in this book, I must demythologize. Having worked with food-service directors now for many years I find that they all have a strawberry endowment. The wise college chef knows that come the spring of the year, even the best diet of institutional food begins to wear on the student palate. Thus the kitchen always saves funds for spring, when lo! steaks or strawberry shortcake begin to appear on the menu with surprising frequency. Peace is sustained.

Football

Chancellor Hutchins of the University of Chicago abolished football on the reported ground that an institution had only two ways to be great: It had to have a great football team or a great president. I don't know about "great," but I am certain that there are more *famous* football coaches than there are famous university presidents. Students seeking a famous institution are more likely to find ready public fame in the athletic arena than elsewhere on campus.

Athletics, as has already been noted, is a latecomer to American colleges and has hardly arrived at all on the worldwide university scene. Faculty often regard athletics—particularly "big-time" athletics—as a hopeless diminishment of the seriousness of the academic task. Nevertheless, athletics is real and present; even the University of Chicago has returned to football.

A full-scale disquisition on college athletics is a task for another tome, but it is worth noting certain aspects of athletics that may influence college culture. Obviously, a very talented student athlete who wants to compete in his or her sport will seek out an institution with a track record. The role of athletics is more likely to be a concern of the modestly talented. One of the major issues is clearly to discover the attention paid to the "minor sports" and—a relatively new concern—women's sports. There are institutions with noted sports names that continue to concentrate on the well-known (and often lucrative) sports. The so-called minor sports (often lifetime sports like tennis or golf) get short shrift, and women's sports (Title IX to the contrary notwithstanding) may be last of all on the attention span. A simple means of assessing the sports program is to count the number of men's and women's sports. Allowing for the basic size of the institution, the more the better.

Big-time football is generally a public-university phenomenon. There are clear exceptions, like Notre Dame and Boston College, but the expense of football usually deters private institutions from Division I competition. (I have always admired the statement of Father Joyce at Notre Dame, who was asked why the university had reversed a historic policy and decided to play in Bowl games. His reply: "For the money, of course. Why would anyone play big-time football except for the money?") The existence of proto-professionalized athletes is not likely to have much immediate effect on an individual student on a state university campus, because of size—not the size of the tackles, the size of the campus population. In some of the more notorious programs, heavy-duty footballers lead an almost wholly segregated life, academically and extracurricularly.

The major effect of big-time sports' presence is as a rallying point for spectators' school spirit. For public institutions supported by a broad taxpayer base, these mammoth sporting events no doubt serve a deep political purpose. Nebraska farmers may not appreciate their philosophy department as much as their football squad. It is a good thing to rally them to the university under any guise. In the private institutions, the importance of intercollegiate athletics is real but over-rated. Outsiders continually claim that successful athletics is a key to happy alumni and successful fund drives. There is very little hard evidence to support this. The main value of athletics has to be for the athletes and for the students who appreciate seeing their friends and acquaintances competing for the school.

Fraternities

Though football can be a controversial subject among educators, even at its very worst it is accepted as a fact of life. Fraternities are another matter. Fraternities get abolished here and there, from time to time, wholesale and retail. Amherst College, after first mandating that all *fraternities* had to admit women, finally decided that they were impossible in any sexual distribution. Williams College abolished its fraternities twenty years ago. Oberlin is proud of the fact that it never had any.

Fraternities are extraordinarily difficult to comprehend since they display such radical historical and geographical disparities. Roughly speaking, Southern and Midwestern fraternities are a psychically different entity from those in the Northeast. Roughly speaking, fraternities then (almost any "then" prior to 1955) are different from fraternities now. Finally, fraternities can and do display the most startling division between rhetoric and reality. Any college official—or parent—reading the goals of almost any fraternity would rush to have a son (and now it could be a daughter) join up. Fraternities do not always shape up to the pledge.

As discussed earlier, fraternities are strictly a youth creation of the nineteenth century, not a structure imposed by the adult authorities. In fact, fraternities were almost universally condemned by faculty and college presidents on a variety of grounds ranging from secrecy to elitism. It is strange, in the contemporary culture, to contemplate that the college authorities condemned societies that were in their origins place getting and adult-oriented.

Because fraternities originally existed so their members could practice the manners of gentlemen at a fashionable club, their charters and codes of behavior would please the most decorous modern dean. In the time since the nineteenth century, however, fraternities, colleges, and life have changed. Colleges are no longer ministerial staging areas. Training young men (and now women) for commercial habits has been taken over by the modern curriculum in finance and economics. Youth culture arrived with a football cheer; the fraternities, weakened by a diminution of their traditional roles of advisers into adulthood, gradually became collegiate with nothing intermediate. With the full-blown youth culture of the post-1960s, fraternities became more and more a last refuge of youth rather than the first step to "adult" status. Alumni adult presence diminished to the point that the only adults likely to be in the house were the permanent cook and, after a noisy weekend, the assistant dean.

This brief history more or less captures the trajectory of fraternities at the older, smaller, private colleges. In the South, where manners still seem to be saluted, fraternities retain some aura of Victorian civilities. At large state institutions fraternities are such ongoing businesses that sheer economic interest will often provide a measure of control.

In assessing the worth of fraternities it is valuable to note that Williams, which abolished fraternities, and Oberlin, which never had them, have created "fraternity substitutes." The small-group social-living concept that is basic to the fraternity is generally admitted on all sides to be an excellence. When fraternities are negatively assessed it is often the mere association with "fraternities!" that is blamed. Alpha Cholera may judge that there is an image of a "frat type" (immortalized in the film *Animal House*) that must be lived up to. The James A. Garfield Society has a more sober set of associations. One might conclude that Williams and others have reinvented the fraternity on a set of assumptions closer to the original model than are many current Greek-letter societies.

Mark Hopkins, Williams's legendary presidential opponent of fraternities, condemned their elitism. That does not seem to be a major problem with most fraternity systems. Law and attitude have changed so decisively that exclusionary practices against Jewish students or blacks are almost everywhere abandoned. There is usually a hierarchy of houses in any campus with an extensive fraternity system, but the egalitarian spirit of modern youth culture—one of its most attractive features—pays little attention to such rankings. The type of house (jocks, Phi Betes) is more likely to be of interest than some presumed status hierarchy. In addition to a welcome change in philosophy, economic determinism helps. Most houses require maximum membership to stay solvent. Rather than exclude, most systems fight to get everybody in somewhere.

One of the most negative things to fall upon fraternities has been the passage of laws raising the legal drinking age to twenty-one. It is almost impossible under those circumstances to avoid having the fraternity house become the local speakeasy. Some campuses have managed to go dry, but it takes peculiarities of local culture to make that stick. To the extent that the fraternity house becomes the illegal public house on campus, its ability—already frail—to maintain the range of its nobler rhetoric is compromised still further.

I have discussed fraternities without mentioning sororities. In my experience, the two institutions are only minimally comparable, for better and for worse. Sororities just aren't the problem that fraternities can be. (I have daughters, recall.) Sororities often do not control real estate. It is common for frats to have a house; sororities may be confined to a room in a college facility. Lacking a house, the possibility of mayhem is diminished. On the other hand, because they lack real estate to maintain, sororities can be more choosy and elitist. It is not that they discriminate on the grounds of race and religion but sororities can afford to be selective and not everyone gets in.

I have had more complaints from angry parents about sorority exclusion than about fraternities.

Fraternities remain a paradox. Most of my academic associates wish they weren't there; but if they weren't there we would invent them. The issue is not fact but the *frat image* on the campus. Are these social additions or theaters for teenage-male dramaturgy? Some of each—at least.

17

Sex and So Forth

When I started my duties as dean of men at Middlebury College the major issue in the office was something called "parietal hours." Today the term is barely comprehended—consigned to the repository of antique words like "antimacassar." "Parietal hours" is an overstuffed term for "visiting hours." (I assume that the Latinate label was intended to show that the issue possessed antiquity and status, not to be dismissed any more than the mortarboard.) The issue, argued year in and year out, was whether women might visit men in their residence halls—and, I assume, vice versa, though that possibility seemed not to be so much envisaged. And if there were to be visiting hours at all, under what conditions. The status of the room door was critical.

In liberated circles beyond Vermont there were some visiting hours and the usual rule was "open door." Sometimes it was specified that the door had to be open at least the width of a book; this was glossed by students as the "matchbook" rule. "Door open or shut?" was much discussed. In a rare moment of administrative inventiveness, I suggested we install Dutch doors in all the dormitories: The students could close one half, the administration would be satisfied with the other half open.

In most colleges the issue of parietal hours has as much currency as my Dutch-door scheme. The world has become so "liberated" that there was a minor fracas at the University of Massachusetts a few years ago when the administration proposed to decoeducationalize the bathrooms. The students protested that this ought not to be done because "coeducational bathrooms were part of the U Mass *tradition!*"

Sexual liberation (by name and of a sort) is a fact of recent life and it is not my purpose here to offer philosophical comment on its virtues or vices. I do think that the effectiveness of parietal hours was oversold by both recalcitrant administrators and eager student petitioners. When I was in college there was a six P.M. rule, which supposedly cleared the dormitories of temptation. It was known as the "no sex after six rule," and led to wonderment among undergraduates about whether the administration believed students were impotent in the afternoon. On the other hand, the absence of parietals has not accomplished quite what the earnest parietal protesters envisaged: romance.

I came to this conclusion but recently, when the president of the student body suggested with some solemnity that the university should run a dating service. What seems to have emerged from open dormitories may be sex or siblinghood, but meeting the right, romantic person still seems to be as difficult as in the days of the eleven P.M curfew. In fact it may be even more difficult. The easy possibilities of dormitory liberation can short-circuit the old-fashioned dating phase, when folks got to know one another in more decorous circumstances.

Sexual liberation has not cured original sin—people still fumble for real companionship even after "the barriers are down"—but it has improved the basic academic idea of a residential campus. The commerce between men and women students postparietals is much easier and more equal than in the past. It has been argued that when men and women are living under the same dormitory roof, in whatever distribution pattern, the incest taboo supervenes on sexuality. Dorm dwellers think of each other as brother and sister, not sexual partners. I find that idea, like "parietals," a bit overstuffed, but I do believe that men and women in the current culture are better able to meet as fellow students and as intellectual peers than in the restricted past. That must be taken as a gain for educational community.

The problem with the new attitude toward sexuality as it works its way across the quad is that bureaucratic restriction is replaced by social coercion. Young people have a keen eye for the sanctions of the adult culture but are generously blind to the force of peer pressure. Being old-fashioned and a parent, I believe, of course, that adult restrictions can be (and should be) liberating from acquiescence to fashion. Old-style parietals and rules in loco parentis were often a refuge from group suasion. With refreshing bravado, students argue that restrictions are a crutch; one just makes up one's mind and says no—the Nancy Reagan method. Perhaps, but it is tough enough to grow up these days without making heroism a routine demand. While we all hope that our friends, our associates, and ourselves are pillars of determined integrity, it is comforting to have external encumbrance as an excuse in weaker moments. (My university has recently begun to hand out buttons which read "No means NO!" If one can't quite say no, the button will.)

The fact that residential facilities are so common at American colleges and universities creates an intensity of peer pressure that contrasts with other ways and days. As noted earlier, President Martin Anderson, good Baptist that he was, objected to dormitories on moral grounds and desired that Rochester students live in family boardinghouses. He would have been happier with the Egyptian expectation that students live at home. European universities have always had powerful student cultures, but they have seldom had any dormitories with the attendant implied doctrine of universitas in loco parentis. Whether it was the medieval student nations or the German

Bruderschaft, European students have created their own brand of culture and/or mayhem not radically different from contemporary American students'—but in the town, not on the quad. In Europe, student life and hijinks are a municipal-police problem, not a campus-life concern. Fretting about sex and the single student is another Calvinist contribution to higher education.

The dominance of student society in establishing appropriate sexual behavior presents two issues for understanding the college scene. First, to what extent can one discover the local "sexual" culture? Despite the earnest efforts of Lisa Birnbach, this is not easy. Colleges seldom advertise on the issue. Most presidents would probably be puzzled about how to describe the mating/dating situation. I do recall attending a solemn meeting of New England college presidents at which the invited president of one of the more "progressive" colleges of the Midwest announced proudly that his college had, after all, pioneered "in making f——ing [not one of the F's mentioned in chapter sixteen] a part of the curriculum"! The then president of Harvard, presiding, took on an expression that matched the portrait of his predecessor Cotton Mather on the wall.

To the best of my knowledge, the progressive president was correct about his campus, which has a particularly ripe reputation. Unless the president is as forthright and knowledgeable as this example, how exactly would one measure this particular interpretation of "hot" campus?

More important than campus culture, certainly, is the sense of individual students on sexual matters. This is a "home truth" if there ever was one. I came to Yale fresh from the quite unliberated tutelage of the Christian Brothers of Ireland. (My high-school education gave me an early appreciation of the Irish taste for terrorism.) It was something of a revelation to discover that the chaps across the hall were posing for a collective oil portrait in naught but jockstraps. (It was a female artist in this case.) Brother O'Hehir would not have approved. It is simple truth that at most college campuses today students will be exposed to at least as surprising a set of sexual attitudes as were displayed by my art-loving hallmates of the 1950s. The issue for the individual is how much of the Christian Brothers, their functional equivalent, and/or family values and expectations will remain determinative.

I have already touched on the modern relation of parents and children on moral values, and the contrast to the nineteenth century. For whatever reasons one may devise, American families are simply not structured in unquestionable moral hierarchies. In a society where children bring suit against their parents for "wrongful birth," one would expect a tattering of old authoritative convention. On the issue of sexual morals, it is not clear what message parents want to send to their college-age children. Parents are as entitled as anyone to be confused by the current state of sexual ethics. When Middlebury was going through the last of many yearly contests over parietals, I volunteered to write to all the parents indicating that we were planning to open visiting hours in the coming year, pending possible reaction from parents. The chairman of the committee examining the matter of parietals was a trustee who was about as conservative as Brother O'Hehir.

I reported to him at the end of the summer on the results of my parental poll. I received *three* letters back from the fifteen hundred sent out. Two parents objected and the third indicated it was about time we caught up with the twentieth century. The trustee capitulated to parental nonpressure.

Had I not engaged in writing this book, I intended to write a short effort on sexual ethics in general. While sex certainly engages our interest, it seldom engages our intellect, and almost never are interest and intellect engaged simultaneously. Even the great Aristotle noted that it is not possible to do metaphysics and have sex at the same time. I have a title for this projected volume: *Sex and So Forth: Trivial Essays on a Profound Subject, or, Profound Essays on a Trivial Subject.* The problem with sex, and with discussing sex with peers or potential freshmen, is that we are not quite able to fix the thing as trivial or profound. There are as many sex tragedies as there are sex comedies. We can't quite make up our minds about sex because it seems to drive us out of our minds in mania and farce.

Discussing the sexual scene with a college student is not one of the parental or presidential moments fondly cherished. My own experience is that the splendid surface virtue of the young, tolerance, makes restrictive discussion on matters sexual nigh unto impossible. Father always sounds like a pre-Freudian fuddyduddy. If I must discuss these matters either with my own daughters or the student population, I confess that I avoid sexual behavior as such in favor of sidling up to the subject by accessing virtues strongly applauded by the young.

I usually plunder the classical curriculum. The Greeks had the notion that there were four central and crucial moral virtues: courage, temperance, justice, and wisdom. Courage is a name for the character trait that gives us "control" over pain; temperance does the same for pleasure. Justice is the virtue for relating to other people. Wisdom is the virtue that relates us to the fundamental nature of reality—God and all such, if any. Of these four virtues, the young (reflecting general culture at the close of the century) are keen on courage and justice. Wisdom is woozy and temperance is nearly a vice. Remember Prohibition! There lies the problem with sexual instruction. Sex has something to do with pleasure. The issue is: Do we need any character trait that "controls" pleasure? There is lots of suggestion that we do not. Impulse buying and impulse bedding are American virtues.

If temperance is a vice and extremism in the pursuit of consumables is a virtue, direct discussion of sexual "control" is an essentially frustrating task. Freud supposedly says it's "all natural" anyhow—like a trendy breakfast cereal, one assumes. The Greeks were on to something, though, with their four virtues. Not only do they cover the territory, but they are interlinked. It is not really possible to fulfill one without some attention to all. The first two, courage and temperance, are ways of "getting the critter's attention." Unless there is a core of personal fortitude that surmounts present pains and pleasures, there is no foundation in the person for the demands of social justice. Since the young are forthright in demanding courage for social justice, I suggest that those themes address the matter of sexual conduct as well. The least one can ask of sexual goings-on is that there be somebody at home during the event. If it is wrong to knuckle under to unpleasantness it can be just as "wrong" to snuggle up to every pleasure. Pain constricts personality; pleasure diffuses. This may not seem like heavy-duty advice, and it will not give infallible instruction as to whether the student should marry, sleep around, or join the Carmelites of the Strict Observance. But if one can put a wedge between desire and doing, it does one vital thing: It makes sexual conduct a matter of choice of self.

Sex is natural (in some sense); selves are chosen (in some sense). No matter how one may argue that this or that sexual activity or pattern of life is "natural" and cannot be avoided, it does not follow that sex is natural the way eating is. There are no "closet digesters." One may *decide* that closet sexuality is bad sexuality, but that is a value choice, not a dictate of biology.

If courage (being somebody) is one route to a semisensible sexual conversation, then justice also has a role. Sex is not only a matter of pleasure; it also can have something to do with other people. On sex and justice, there is likely to be a differential conversation with males and females in the family. I have endured more than one male fracas in fraternities or dorms in which "sexual harassment"—to use a mild phrase— was the issue; it seems clear that in the minds of males in collectivity there remains a serious misperception about justice. (Individuals are less likely to be unjust than masses and mobs. When I am acting as a single person, it is a lot harder to pretend that the other is not also a person. Collectives are not so careful in their perceptions.) The fault in these fracas events seems hard for the participants to comprehend. "But she agreed!" is the usual excuse. Perhaps—though alcohol usually assists the decision. "She agreed" is a nonexcuse if the behavior is exploitative, and it usually is. People just can't agree to give away their worth and it is a responsibility of justice not to agree to such undignifying agreements. Whatever the final moral assessment of these incidents, the atmosphere on college campuses is very intolerant of "boys will be boys." The advent of women on formerly all-male campuses, the women's liberation movement, and the attitude of the public law toward rape, all place male students involved in such events in very serious trouble.

For women students the advice is milder. The principal advice is likely to be: Don't be a victim. Again relying on courage and justice to do something positive for temperance, one underlines the fact that it is always necessary to *be somebody*. As long as the woman maintains a clear sense of self-worth, it is impossible to suggest in suggestive situations that being a victim is okay by me. Going along with the crowd is not "being somebody."

A final deep concern for female students is "woman as victim" from attack. A few recent tragic events on a few college campuses have raised concern even in the legislatures. The Commonwealth of Pennsylvania has been persuaded to pass a law that would require colleges and universities to inform parents on request about the incidence of serious crime on their premises. On many campuses, feminist critics already accuse officials of covering up information about rape and assault so as not to alarm potential applicants. It would be foolish to pretend that the modern open campus does not create situations of hazard that did not exist in more restrictive times. Dorm mothers guarded and locked the doors. Bad things come from outside, but sometimes from within the campus community itself. However, after all the statistics are collected and published they show that the college campus remains a reasonably safe environment. Insofar as campus-security and municipal-police records are concerned, serious crime on a campus is quite rare. Of course not everything is reported, particularly underreported are complex individual situations between students that involve some assent, some coercion, and lots of personal trauma. The pain measurement would certainly go beyond the measure of the police blotter. But for sheer danger from predatory strangers, the campus is not a hostile environment.

18

Getting In, On, and Out

I n some families picking a college has become a more solemn decision than picking a spouse—at least if the divorce statistics are to be believed. The legendary dad who pleaded to have his son become a Princeton alumnus with or without a Princeton education seems to have been more wedded to Princeton-in-the-family than any other, lesser domestic arrangements. It is a simple life mistake to be so tied to a single school, no matter how glittering. The general truth is that an excellent outcome from education can be had at a large range of institutions glorious and unknown.

If only Old Ivy or New Tech will be acceptable then the best advice is to imitate John Oznot. Mr. Oznot was an applicant to Princeton in the sixties, who had SAT scores of 600 plus, quarterbacked his high-school football team, and appeared at the admissions interview in a letter sweater carrying a copy of Shakespeare. He was admitted without question but, unhappily, Oznot was not: He was a hoax concocted by the undergraduate who impersonated him at the interview. The prankster knew the tricks of admission and presented scholastic honors, athletic prowess, and a poetic soul all in one paragon. The combination will get you admitted almost anywhere.

Continuing the course in "physics of collegiate entities," I move from considering collegiate degrees Kelvin (hot, cool, not-so-hot) to the specific gravity of the decision for A, B, C, and Safety School. If it is worthwhile to moderate temperature, I also think it wise to reduce weightiness. I do not mean that Any Old U. will do. Far from it. But once there is a reasonable range of institutions one can have sensible assurance that genuine education can emerge. A quality list could be drawn up from the effables discussed in earlier chapters, since they are the aspects that influence outcome of education. Once the effable list is in order one can turn to the other F's and do the ranking. But even the last school on the F list will probably be an excellent place for academics—and even fun.

Assuming that the applicant is not Oznot, there are rational factors and externalities that influence college admissions. The rational factors are simple and straightforward. Academic aptitude is the heaviest counter. Despite the trauma and editorial attacks on SAT and ACT scores and all that, the most important factor for almost all admissions offices is the high-school record. The most important part of that record is important courses with good grades. Colleges prefer bread-and-butter courses rather than academic canapés. English, history, math, and science, not choir II and advanced cheerleading.

After the academic credentials, factorial weight diminishes rapidly. The next-most-important consideration is likely to be something like intellectual energy. If an applicant can demonstrate on top of the A's and B's genuine curiosity and a robust interest in life, the world, and college study, that will be a strong addition to the record. Energy can be inferred from the list of extracurricular activities, but too long a list is likely to suggest diffusion and/or padding. Not all extracurricular activities are intelligible or impressive to the admissions officer. I had to be taught what a "candy striper" meant: a hospital assistant. I wondered, then, about the student who listed herself

as a "candy stripper." My favorite extracurricular activity was
that of the young man who listed his principal one as "girl-
friend"—though only in his sophomore and senior years.

Recommendations from teachers who know the student well
are welcome; recommendations from impressive next-door
neighbors who know the student from lawn mowing are less
than worthless and are likely to annoy the admissions office.
Character reference in general is not of much value. One just
does not know how to evaluate the claim "whitest soul east of
the Mississippi River." Certain extracurricular activities are
strong contenders. Star athletics is too obvious to avoid mention. On the other hand, unless one is a genuine star (and
probably being recruited) putting faith in athletics for admission
can be a mistake. Athletics admits are scrupulously reviewed
by the athletics coaches, so there is a true weeding-out process.
Potential poets are not usually so scrutinized by the resident
literary faculty. Among the extracurricular activities most likely
to counterweight a C in chemistry is music—but not all music.
I was certain one year when reading admissions folders at
Bucknell that the campus would be one large guitar jangle.
Serious drummers are a serious problem because colleges have
a terrible time finding a secluded practice place. There are
many high-school bands and many trombone players therein;
there are few high-school orchestras, and most colleges are
eager for any string player they can obtain (not guitar, as noted).
A rather poor third, behind athletics and violin playing, is
"editor of . . ." The ratio of high-school editors to active college journalists is so low, either by election or selection, that
an admissions officer simply cannot judge whether the editor
of the Keokuk H.S. *Bugle* will perform as such in college.

Choice of major can be an important factor in admission,
particularly if the major is one of the less favored. I have often
thought that the rational (and shrewd) strategy for the ambitious
would be a major in classics. A strong application written in
the best Silver Latin would probably gain instant admission
not only to Harvard but to the French Academy. Not only are
classics majors even more desired than violinists, in any college

founded before 1900 there are many prizes left over (and few contestants) for the best essay on Horace; these prizes can be garnered by the ambitious student of Latin. One could finance a good part of education on prize essays alone. Philosophy, physics, mathematics, even history, fall in the less-favored majors and will gain the attention of the admissions office. (The number of history majors in the United States has declined by 50 percent over the last ten years.)

The percentage of humanities majors in general has fallen to below 5 percent, so any choice in that area will catch the college's admitting eye. Lest anyone think I recommend these majors as an admissions ploy, let me say that I actually believe that they are among the very best majors available. The problem is that they are difficult. Classics, for instance, is valuable because it teaches an *anatomy* for language. I trace the decline in writing skills to the abandonment of Latin in the high schools. Philosophy, rather than the most impractical of subjects, is in my judgement immensely useful. We spend most of life arguing with somebody (boss, spouse, customer) about something, and philosophy is training in argument. Undergrad philosophers are a breeze for law school.

After the obvious—academics plus energy plus extracurricular activity—there are the important externalities. Some research at one admissions office discovered that more people were being admitted from the first half of the alphabet than from the second. The reason was obvious. If you start to read from Adams and go on to Zickl, by the time you get on into the T's you have already admitted enough and you now have to deadmit D to admit S. So, the Wyschgorods of the world should check to make sure that admissions folders are read randomly.

Aside from the accidents of the admissions-office routine, the most important other externality is externality itself: Is the applicant different, outside the normal applicant profile? Thus, the more "external" candidates are to the place, the better chance for admission. Not everyone can move to Alaska, of course, just for admissions purposes. There are other externalities. Everyone wants to broaden the traditional racial and ethnic mix on campus, so there is a definite plus for admission in that degree of difference. Farm children and daughters and sons of blue-collar workers are underrepresented at the most selective colleges, and thus are likely to get special attention.

In drawing up the list, the most difficult selection is the "safety school." It is simply impossible not to be admitted to college in America if you really want to go. The most rational safety-school determination is a place with one (to the candidate) horrendous externality. Location will do. Case Western Reserve is a noble institution, in Cleveland. (A beautiful site next to a superb symphony hall and the distinguished Cleveland Museum of Fine Art.) Catholic University of America is on the "unfashionable" side of town from hot Georgetown. Grinnell has a lovely bank building designed by Louis Sullivan, an extraordinarily interesting college, and miles of verdant corn. The most common mistake in college decisions is turning down academic excellence because there is too much local smog or alfalfa.

If it is a mistake to choose a college for its fake Gothic or real rhododendrons, it compounds the mistake to stay at a wrong choice. Thus it is curious how little students think about transfer. There probably are more divorces per marriage than there are transfers per college admit. This is a tribute to the quality of colleges: They do satisfy student needs. On the other hand, a significant number of students get a dose of reality after the romance of the admissions process. They discover that the college has the wrong social atmosphere, or their planned major is, for this college, a weak one, or they can't get their hands on a cyclotron. America has the most forgiving educational system in the world. A distinguished researcher worried about the dropouts from the California system of higher education concluded that students weren't lost to education— they simply migrated from Sacramento to Davis to UCLA to Riverside to . . . Her final conclusion was that the only dropouts from the California system were the deceased.

The California system of university centers, state universities, colleges, community colleges, and whatever else remains to be invented is a particularly ripe case of academic range. One can go up and down the chromatic scale of academic class and clout without ever leaving the state. Not all states range from the most modest local opportunity to a world-class university like Berkeley, but many states come close, and the entire academic enterprise in America is a remarkably open-textured system. Students may start at Siwash and end at Stanford. European and Asian universities offer a sharp contrast. If one fails to score strongly on the school-leaving examination, the road to any higher education may be almost permanently closed. America forgives multitudes of scholastic sins.

I would not wish to leave the impression that the signpost to American higher education reads "ENTER ANYWHERE." It is remarkable that people do enter almost anywhere and end up summa cum laude from *somewhere*. Intelligence and true grit are necessary ingredients for upscaling, but it is done. Within the undergraduate years ease of transfer from institution to institution is variable according to sector (public or private) and selectivity. As noted, the California public system is extraordinarily open-textured to the ambitious. Private prestige institutions are much more difficult for undergraduates to transfer into; transfers often depend on exceptional talent and specialized educational need. Transfer from excellent liberal-arts *colleges* to leading research *universities* is not so difficult, however, if the student can demonstrate the need and ability to benefit from the greater range and depth of the university curriculum.

The most common transfer point for students is the end of sophomore year. Most institutions require that to receive their degree the student must complete two years' work at the college or university of transfer. Although rational transfers should be encouraged, the fact is that most transfers are as subject to romantic prompting as the initial decision. Without a doubt the most statistically common source of transfer is the presence of a boy or girl interest at the transfer institution. Another common reason given for transfer is "dissatisfaction with the social life"; this usually means that one does not have a boy or girl interest locally either. A number of students simply transfer unhappiness with them from quad to quad.

In addition to getting in and getting around (to other places) there is getting out (actually graduating). Having spent four years being convinced that I would never graduate (surely a great university would some day discover my manifold, manifest incompetences), I would like to offer a reassuring word based on experience and survival. It is very difficult to flunk out of the contemporary college.

One of the most amusing parts of being dean of dropouts was dealing with the Princeton grading system as it was then. It was the only system ever devised that not only had *five* passing grades (most places have only four: A, B, C, D) it had *two* (count 'em, two) failing grades. There was a regular failure (a 6) and a sort of "failure with distinction" (7), called "flagrant neglect." A 6 was a good old honest college-try failure; "flagrant neglect" displayed a contumelious attitude toward academic tasks. One never showed up in class, handed in no homework, and absented oneself from the final exam. Two citations for flagrant neglect were automatic dismissal. Naturally such a cumbersome grading system led to all sorts of puzzlement about what it all meant. I frequently found myself explaining to a baffled outside inquirer that "flagrant neglect" was not the same as "in flagrante." The registrar always included an interpretation sheet with transcripts, explaining that a Princeton 2 + was really everyone else's A − and that a 3 − was more or less a C and that one couldn't be sure that a 4 was really a D at all. One exasperated recipient of the explanation sent back a classic reply: "Congratulations, you have made a trivial subject profound."

I mention this archaic grading machine because on the whole it seems to me that it takes the functional equivalent of flagrant neglect to flunk out of college these days. Princeton no longer uses the "group" grading system (as it was called) but, more important, most college faculties have abandoned prior assumptions about undergraduate grading altogether. Not only do college faculties not string students out from 1 to 7, they don't even use the A, B, C system, as one might assume. Grade inflation has become a well-recognized national phenomenon, which has accompanied declining SAT scores and rising complaints about the attained competencies of graduates. What has happened is that the assumptions of graduate-school grading have descended upon undergraduate grading. Graduate grading runs along the same five-level system as undergraduate grading. A common package would be Excellent, Very Good, Good, Pass, and Fail. The problem is that, as every graduate student clearly understands it, Good is Bad, Pass is Fail, and Fail is Instant Death. Translate those graduate assumptions into undergraduate marks and one assumes that only A and B are worthy grades at all. A grade of C is only tolerable, and anything below that indicates that the admissions office needs to tighten up again. The net effect of the graduate-grading assumptions has been to raise all grades and make flunking out of college a willful act of flagrant neglect. Those who get in, get out.

19

The Major Issue
of Minorities

While I was serving at Middlebury College, an earnest collegiate historian concluded that Middlebury had graduated the first African-American ever to receive a B.A. It may be symbolic that his name was Twilight. African-Americans have been in the twilight of American higher education for most of its long history. It wasn't even of much importance to research one's minority graduates. After all, there weren't many at most places, and was it all that important, anyhow? After the civil-rights movements of the 1960s it became very important. It is even more important today.

Much of this book has been addressed to the differences between colleges past and universities present. Any discussion of African-Americans in higher education is likely to move into higher education future. As of the year this book is being written, the number of high-school graduates throughout the country is plummeting, and it will continue to decline for about five more years. Around 1995 the high-school graduating classes begin to expand once more. But the student world post-1995 will be very different. Minorities will be majorities—at least in many states. If one takes the U.S. government definition of "under-represented minorities"—blacks, Hispanics, Asians, Native Americans—minorities *already* are the majority population in the California university system. The post-1995 college student bodies will be more black and more Hispanic—or at least they *should* be.

There is no doubt that in some aggregate sense future college populations will be more ethnically and racially diverse. What that does *not* say is that the kind of colleges discussed in this book will be more diverse. It may be that the black and Hispanic populations will be found in the community colleges but remain heavily underrepresented in the senior colleges and universities of the land. The fact that the number of blacks and Hispanics receiving bachelor's degrees has declined in the past ten years is not a happy portent. The fact that the number of blacks and Hispanics pursuing advanced *academic* degrees (Ph.D.'s) is minuscule offers a grim forecast for future faculties.

When I took American history in college, we read David Potter's *People of Plenty*, an account of the American experience. Professor Potter, who taught the class, argued that the large story of American history was of relative affluence. However, he noted on page one that while this was the big story line it did not at all apply to blacks and Native Americans. It may be that a text on college myths and university realities also misses the minority populations. All this delicacy about the liberal arts, service and saga, and the role of fraternities may be of some curious interest to Deerfield graduates, but it may mean something less than zero to young people from Bedford-Stuyvesant. The present chapter is addressed to that discrepancy—I hope for all the races and nationalities of the contemporary campus and the quad-to-come.

Before addressing this most difficult topic, I want to attempt some clarifications and make some apologies before the fact. This chapter is largely directed at African-American issues in higher education. By labeling this "African-American" I immediately date the book to sometime after 1988. When David Potter wrote *People of Plenty*, he referred to "negroes" and "Indians" as the groups excluded from affluence. That dates his book to the 1950s. A good mid-1960s book would probably have confidently spoken of "black" issues. Jesse Jackson's championing "African-American" in his presidential campaign seems to have turned a tide for this (quite accurate) designation.

The matter of name is, however, relatively insignificant when one considers some of the more complex and potentially misleading rallying words in the field. As already noted, "minority" may turn out to be a simple failure to do arithmetic as "minorities" come to outnumber Anglos. "Underrepresented" certainly is accurate but may raise the question whether certain minorities are "overrepresented" (the concern of the Asian community is that talented students are being denied access to prestigious educational institutions because of some overall quota scheme, stated or implied, in admission.) Finally, there is what I regard as the most problematic word in the lexicon of educational goals: "diversity."

I had the privilege of being the chair of an accreditation team at Bryn Mawr College in the fall of 1988. The most vexing issue on the campus by all reports was "diversity." Having read all the studies and spent several days on the campus, it struck me that the search for "diversity" was seriously misleading. For many years, Bryn Mawr has had an enviable record of admitting foreign students. I have seldom seen a more "diverse" student body. Students from every continent, race, and religion were there in significant numbers. Buddhists could argue with Sabras from Israel; Brazilians encountered mainland Chinese at the lunch counter. What were *under*-represented at Bryn Mawr—as at most selective colleges—were American citizens of African descent. I am not certain that Bryn Mawr needed more worldwide diversity; it did need (and want) more American citizens of color.

While it may be a turn of broadmindedness to encapsulate the recruitment of African-Americans under the "diversity" label, I believe it is always dangerous to create vagueness when specificity is required. If "diversity" were only a polite label, I suppose it could be tolerated, but the word can also lead colleges, their administrators, faculty, and students down some unpromising pathways.

We have been so deluged with demands for diversity that it might be well to step back for a moment and ask what *sort* of diversity we really have in mind. This is a particularly important issue for colleges. When "diversity" has been used in a large, ideological sense in the curriculum, the impact has been inversely proportional to the controversy. It is alleged that the curriculum is ideologically racist or ethnic European and needs to be expanded to the "diverse" demands of world culture. While there is a good argument for learning the local topography before venturing to other continents, the general notion of diversified ideas in the university curriculum can hardly be defeated. The problem is that at best such "diversity" will affect only a small proportion of the basic curriculum of almost any college. As one might expect, the major curricular changes reflecting the diversity of human ways are in the humanities. At last count less than 5 percent of college students majored in the humanities. Even if one extends "diversity" to the social sciences, the number of students choosing courses that readily admit of diversity will remain quite small. When it comes to some of the most fundamental university studies—and areas where the need for "minorities" is most pressing—diversity becomes marginal to the vanishing point. The mathematical underpinnings of the natural and social sciences seem to admit no diversity by race and ideology.

Mathematics offers an interesting issue for "diversity," not because there is some race-oriented algebra but because math is an area where diversity-of-learning-culture may be all-important. Professor Uri Treisman, at Cal Berkeley, became very concerned several years ago that African-American students had deviantly poor records in elementary calculus, the gateway math for all the sciences. He examined the standard rationales for poor performance: bad high-school education, low SATs, poor motivation, lack of parental support, economic deprivation. He could make none of the hypotheses work. Students with good high-school grades and high SATs seemed to have as many problems as students with poor preparation and low scores. In desperation, he started to follow the students around through the day to discover how they studied. He also followed Asian students, since they were doing extraordinarily well in the same courses. What he found was a distinct diversity in learning style. The Asians studied in groups—they referred to them as "work gangs"—while the black students tended to work alone. By cohorting students and insisting that the cohorts attack honors-level calculus problems, Treisman has turned disaster into success for his minority students.

It is very likely that learning cultures are diverse and that unless colleges are attentive to some basic family, ethnic, and racial learning cultures they will fail to teach the "new" populations. James Comer's studies of performance by minorities in the early school years strongly suggest that it is the lack of certain "social skills" (negotiation, compromise) that makes the social structure of the school so difficult to traverse. Search for diverse style, however, cannot disguise the fact that physics is physics is physics for all that political science is not just the *Federalist*, but also Frederick Douglass.

When "diversity" is used as the rallying word for African-American presence, it seems to me both very right and very wrong. Consider the other significant "underrepresented minority," Hispanics. Hispanics have certainly shared much of the economic and social deprivation of the African-American population, but in the university culture "Hispanicism" poses a very different issue. Spanish is, after all, a major *European* language. In so far as the university is a distinctly European invention—and it is—Spain is a major participant. Hispanics can immediately retrieve a comprehensive and extant linguistic, political, and artistic heritage, either Peninsular or in the Western hemisphere, which fits at every juncture with the broad lines of the European assumptions of the university.

In comparison to Hispanics, then, *African*-Americans present a formidable diversity. African linguistic and political roots are radically different from the European experience. Many of the principal languages lack a long written history to be recovered. Finally, by accident of materials and climate, great works of African art have proved perishable. With the clear exception of the Benin bronzes, most major artifacts from Africa are of quite recent date. In sum, Hispanics can easily pick up the threads of their background culture in American universities; African-Americans cannot. All the more reason, I would argue, for special attention to the African heritage— because it really *is* diverse.

At the same time, however, while universities rightly may seek diversity in Africa, the African-American is, de facto, probably more American than African. Having been divorced from African roots by centuries of oppression, recovery of that heritage is likely to be subtle and indirect, as in the echoes of Africa in jazz. The dominant *experience* for African-Americans has been American—specifically being the American outcast. Blacks have been defined, for the worse, in an American set of expectations from which they were excluded. The aspirations of African-Americans are not so much diverse as denied. The civil-rights struggle centered on black people obtaining what whites had all along: the vote; education; the right to eat at any lunch counter, sleep in any hotel, and travel without segregation. One could argue that the current demand of blacks is a pure American wish list: a job, a decent home, safety in the streets. Nothing very "diverse" there.

The civil-rights movement that discovered Alexander Twilight created a new history for African-Americans in regard to higher education. It was clearly the right moral turn for history, but it was a novel event in the American history of educating deprived populations. Like all really new things in history, it has proved difficult to absorb.

If the black experience in higher education is likely to prove different from the Hispanics', it is worth comparing the black situation with past precedent. It was both fitting and ironic that Bryn Mawr College should be agitated about "diversity." Bryn Mawr was founded to provide higher education of uncompro-

mising standards—equal to those of Johns Hopkins—to a deprived minority that could neither vote nor receive advanced
degrees in American colleges. The women's colleges—Bryn
Mawr not least—served the de facto (and sometimes de jure)
deprived. Women have not been the only group excluded from
select higher education. Catholics and Jews also found
themselves less than welcome at the establishment, all-too-
Protestant colleges, so they created their own. In time, these
outposts of the deprived have flourished, become very significant centers of higher education, and—in the case of some
of the women's institutions (Vassar) and the "religious" universities (Georgetown, Notre Dame, Brandeis) have "diversified" beyond their original constituent student bodies.

Specialized institutions for the excluded were also created
for the sons and daughters of slavery: the historically black
colleges, Tuskegee, Fisk, Spelman, and so on. In the longer
run of history one might have had every expectation that the
black colleges would have followed something like the trajectory of the Catholic institutions "from backwater to main-
stream" and, in several significant cases, from modest
educational achievement to the first rank or near it. History
did not work that way. In the first place, the African-American
population, despite enormous personal sacrifice, just did not
have the resources in the general society of either the women's
schools or even the most lowly of the immigrant religious
populations. It was not possible in the timespan allotted to
"grow" the dedicated black liberal-arts institutions into major
university centers. The civil-rights movement truncated the
"natural" development when the old, exclusionary, establishment institutions began to raid the students (and faculty) of
the black colleges.

The recruitment, then, of African-American students (and
faculty) to the main-line white campuses has been revolution-
ary, not evolutionary. History has a hard time with revolutions.
Laws change but cultures persist. If one accepts the analysis
above, African-Americans may seem to the universities, and
feel to themselves, peculiarly alienated, more alienated than

women, Hispanics, Catholics, or Jews. The university is a place of diversity of ideas, cultures, and styles. It should not have great problems adjusting to distant religions and strange customs. The alienation of African-Americans at dominantly white institutions is something else: A "majority" university is an American institution including those defined as "the Americans excluded." Hispanics can seek refuge in Europe; Vietnamese are really different; blacks are very much *the same* (Americans) but with a heritage of exclusion. No wonder there are racial tensions on majority campuses.

Many current studies indicate that black student performance diminishes in white environments. In a controlled experiment, an all-black class and a mixed-race class of matched ability were set common math problems. The all-black class performed significantly better than the mixed-race class. One can only suppose that the presence of white Americans sends a continuing message to black Americans: You don't belong here. If someone has the sense that they don't belong here (in calculus), it is no surprise that they underperform.

The moral of the current situation for African-American students, higher education, and the society is easy to draw, complex to act on. African-Americans must lose once and for all any taint of "exclusion." The immediate practical advice to blacks might well be to seek out all-black institutions that continue a record of excellence under adversity. Studies indicate that black students do better at such institutions. But directing black students to black institutions is impractical on the large and in the long run. If higher education is to serve the African-American population adequately it will have to be through mixed-race institutions, simply because they constitute the vast majority of colleges. But if this is the *practical* solution it is abundantly clear that the majority institutions have yet to create the social conditions that maximize the great potential of the black student.

Most African-American students are served on mixed-race campuses—and despite all the problems they can and do succeed. Some succeed by black cohorting, others find ways of negotiating the dominantly white culture. Most colleges and universities have "minority affairs" offices, which attend to the special concerns of blacks, Hispanics, and Native Americans. The task of these special programs is extraordinarily difficult: how to help students adjust without somehow suggesting that they are permanently maimed and thus need perpetual help. My African-American vice-president for students has it right when he welcomes students by telling them that they are young, healthy, bright, and future leaders of the nation. Amen!

20

What's It Cost?

C ollege in America has *always* cost too much. This claim can be verified by simple memory. If the reader is over forty, did his or her parents graduate from college? The chances are good that they did not. Prior to World War II (and as late as 1941) less than 6 percent of the U.S. population had graduated from college. The dominant reason that more people did not go to college was cost.

In contrast, the parents of contemporary applicants are products of the post–World War II period when a decisive change occurred in college entrance and graduation. The single great event was the G.I. Bill, which awarded an educational bonus to veterans. For the first time a very large proportion of the population found higher education wholly affordable. If the G.I. Bill was the initiatory event, all sorts of other changes occurred in tandem and in consequence. The state systems expanded, enlarged their curricula, and upgraded. Inexpensive public education was financially, geographically, and program-matically available. Private higher education became more broadly based as the elite schools turned aside from traditional feeder prep schools and sought a wider geographic and economic spectrum of students. They were assisted financially by growing programs of state and federal grants and loans to students. Less than fifty years after the war we find that over 50 percent of the high-school-age population goes on to some type of postsecondary education.

The tuition charges at the most expensive private colleges and universities have in the past decade taken a slightly greater proportion of disposable family income than in the historic past. So, college costs—*some* college costs—have risen. The modest rise in cost, however, is quite out of proportion with the popular and political clamor about high-cost education. It is the clamor that needs to be explained as much as the cost.

The G.I. Bill and its attendant phenomena created the "high cost of college." More or less. In the days when collegegoing was rare and for the rich, the perennial high cost of higher learning was a problem of marginal public attention. Given today's collegegoing rate, 1941's statistics on college graduates seem a fact from an underdeveloped sub-Saharan principality. My father and mother were born at the end of the nineteenth century, and in 1900 the college-graduate population was less than 2 percent. It was uncommon for lawyers or even doctors to be college trained—only ministers and teachers bothered. Few people worried about the high cost of a good education that even fewer people wanted, or that was regarded as so far above economic reach as to be beyond even envy. It isn't really worth a lot of time stewing about the fact that one does not own the Kohinoor Diamond. The postwar era made it "diamonds all around."

I mention these historical facts only to lessen shock and/or resentment when one confronts the costs of higher education. Although higher education may impair the family bank balance, it ought not to create a new class enemy: the professorial exploiter of the working wage-earner. Higher education has been a *relatively* costly business all along. (It is also worth noting that the high cost of complex higher education is a world problem, not a local American phenomenon. It is equally interesting that our very successful economic competitors from the Pacific Rim are extraordinarily anxious to finance their nationals' attendance at America's leading research universities. Somebody knows a good financial deal.)

Before proceeding further in discussing college cost it is important to make one vital clarification. When people talk about the cost of higher education in newspaper headlines set in thirty-point type, they are always talking about *tuition*. What interests the news reader is the cost to the consumer. The cost of education has another meaning, which college presidents worry about: the cost of *providing* the education. What does it cost to hire a faculty, fire the furnace, and dust the books in the library? Every year the president or his ghostwriter attempts a letter to parents explaining that the costs of providing the service have a relation to the costs to the consumer. On the evidence of my return mail, these letters are singularly ineffective in making the connection. Not that one gets that many complaints. Tuition escalation has now joined death and taxes as an inevitability.

Having discussed public and private education and the attendant high cost of private education, it is important to emphasize that the cost of providing services is substantially the same in comparable institutions across the sectors. In short, it costs Berkeley as much to produce a Ph.D. as it does Stanford. The difference in tuition and fees is due to the substantial subsidy to public education that is contributed by taxpayers. One is likely to hear complaints about state grants to students at private institutions because such grants are "taxpayer subsidies to the rich." This is clearly a misperception. The taxpayer contributes a bundle to pay the *cost of providing services* to a student at SUNY or the Cal system. The student who goes to Stanford or Harvard or Chicago costs the same, but he or she pays a substantial part of the cost. Private higher education is a bargain to the tax system. Instead of worrying about subsidizing rich kids at private schools (where they have to pay substantial fees from their own resources) it might be as well to worry about subsidizing rich kids at public universities. Public higher education is a substantial middle-class welfare benefit.

A second clarification vital in discussing "the high cost of higher education" is that the headlines only refer to a very small percentage of the total universe of colleges. It is *Harvard's* tuition that hits the headlines. The Ivies; a selection of the major private research universities; the most distinguished liberal-arts colleges; and a few special engineering and science institutes—about fifty out of 3,300 institutions—are *really* expensive. Even if one confines oneself to private colleges—the ones that live on tuition and thus charge "high" prices—these only constitute 20 percent of the colleges in the country. The other 80 percent are low-priced state institutions, which offer education at fees that start low and go all the way down to zero. Nor is it fair to regard the private 20 percent of colleges and universities as the price busters. Many private colleges have very modest tuitions—especially when compared to the fifty top-priced.

One further clarification on cost to the consumer, that is, tuition: No one attending any institution (public or private) needs to believe the "sticker price." There are so many forms of financial aid: school scholarships, state grants, Federal Opportunity Grants, discounted loans, fraternal-organization merit scholarships, athletic free rides, and what not, that the financial-aid officer has become a college official with expertise befitting a Philadelphia tax lawyer. The problem may not be so much the lack of funds as the complexity of programs (and the attendant bureaucratic forms) that generate financial assistance.

The previous paragraph is bound to elicit protest. There is a definite "middle-class squeeze" when it comes to funding college education. For those below a certain income level there are many programs of assistance, though the final bill still amounts, in most cases, to a considerable financial burden on the family. For those above a certain income, the cost is not an issue. It is the family in the middle, not "poor enough" for welfare, not rich enough for "wealth," that appears caught. The problem is the necessary imperfection of the financial-aid system. The assignment of financial assistance to families is at least as sensible as the income-tax system. A number of "arbitrary" assumptions are made in calculating need. It may surprise the general reader to know that families with incomes over $100,000 can receive financial assistance given enough untoward circumstances—like having four children in college at the same time—but it remains true that the "middle class" *feels* most left out of the set of discounts and set-asides that determine the final out-of-pocket cost for the typical financial-aid recipient.

I cannot repair the necessary arbitrariness of the financial-aid system, but I will say some words about why we all *feel* less capable of meeting college costs. Even after all the necessary clarifications about tuition versus cost of services, sticker price, and cash out of pocket, the fact of the matter is that college was, is, and will no doubt remain a major financial issue for students and families. I have attempted to show that the high cost of higher education is not a recent malignant invention, like disco dancing; but some factors both in the cost of service and cost to families are recent and must be noted if one is to derive any perspective on this high(ly) charge(d) issue.

Why does higher education really *cost more than when Grandfather went to college? Why does higher education* seem *to cost more than when Mother went there too?* After all the historical wisdom one can muster there is just no doubt that higher education in recent years has been a more expensive product than traditionally. Certain reasons are relatively easy to understand, and generally win sympathy. Everyone appreciated in the period of high inflation—particularly inflation in basic services—that it was necessary to raise tuition to cover the oil bill. What seems exasperating is that the price keeps rising even after general inflation has moderated. The reason for the escalation lies in two areas. One, higher education is simply *better* than it was. Two, consumers drive the price up.

Is education really better than it was when Grandfather

found it so expensive he went to work in the mill instead? My grandfather did not go to the mill; he actually went to college. As described earlier, Grandfather not only went to college; he actually became a college teacher. (Given the high cost of college education [about $50 a year tuition] he thought a job at a college was the only way he could afford to educate his five children.)

With all due respect to Grandfather, it doesn't appear that he knew very much about the subject matter he was supposed to teach. As noted, sociology hadn't been invented when he was in college, so he had to translate ministerial concern with sinners into sociological science. I am certain that no one with similar training would be appointed today at Ripon to teach the subject. Contemporary university critics may complain about "academic specialization," but it is unlikely that anyone would really want to go back to the ministerial amateur. The academic trades have clearly been substantially improved in skill, knowledge, and power to influence thought and action. Knowledge—particularly specialized knowledge that requires extended training to acquire—demands a price. No one needs to pay to discover today's weather: Open the window. But tomorrow's weather? You need a trained meteorologist. Ministers may have believed that the poor in spirit are blessed and most, like Grandfather, kept such blessedness in spirit and material circumstance; modern professors believe that "the laborer is worthy of his hire."

The underlying cost push on college education has been the continual professionalization of faculties. Professionals expect to be compensated as professionals in a manner commensurate with the value of their skills. The underlying escalation of college costs is not unlike the other area in the economy where costs have run ahead of general inflation: medical care. When doctors knew as much about medicine as my grandfather knew about sociology, it was divine justice that costs were more moderate. Paying to be leeched is nowhere near as costly (or as worth it) as lithotripsy.

From time to time one hears claims that colleges and universities could be run less expensively. This is absolutely true. The question for those thinking about real cost-cutting is the character of consumer demand. Not only has sociology gotten better since Grandfather, there are a lot more -ologies out there, which respond to consumer demand. The old-style college at which Grandfather was educated concentrated on the classical curriculum discussed at length earlier. The assemblage of high-minded materials culled from the Greeks and the Romans produced eloquence for preachers and classical prose for politicians. (Blessedly. Imagine the Declaration of Independence in "business English": "When in the ongoing process of personnel interactions it becomes appropriate for one subsidiary corporation to 'lay it on the line'—so to speak . . .") The classical curriculum was not only eloquent, it was cheap. No labs for Lucretius. The curriculum was also permanent over a long cycle—since Diocletian, perhaps. Concentration on a permanent, limited curriculum constricts costs remarkably. St. John's College in Annapolis, Maryland, with its classical curriculum fixed over four years should be the least expensive college in America. (If it is not, that is because generalist faculties in a world of specialists are rare, valuable, and expensive.)

The more unidirectional an educational institution, the more economical—and if it can stay out of high-tech hardware and stick to Hellenistic software, it can be remarkably inexpensive. The problem is that most educational consumers want something other than Horace and highmindedness. One of my clients at Princeton was a young man who had literally withdrawn from the life of the university, to secrete himself in the computer building. When the doors were locked at night he hid in the bathroom. In that era, the computer building was *the* computer building. The idea that one day you could secrete the computer in your bathroom rather than the other way around was unthinkable. A very large number of parents and students are as avid for many computers on campus as my long-ago student was for Princeton's sole instrument.

The proliferation of curricula—and especially the prolifer-

ation of the necessary scientific and technical curricula—
brings to colleges a train of costs that were scarcely imagined
even in Mother's and Father's time. Parents and applicants
want those services. Costs rise and tuitions pay for them.

There is another consumer-demand push on educational
cost-of-service: the so-called "administrative costs." Anyone
who surveys the staffs of colleges then and now has noted a
remarkable rise in the number of administrators. Most people
who compile such figures share the faculty philosophy that
there are only two kinds of administrators: those who hinder
and those who fail to hinder. If only we could get rid of all
the bureaucrats then we could save money and get to the real
business of education in the libraries and labs.

Would that it were so simple. One could start with a brand-
new invention in administration, an invention already mentioned: the financial-aid officer. In the 1930s such a person
was as undiscovered as a quark. Not even parents would be
likely to wish this office to disappear. And so the argument
might go across a range of student services that are unlikely to
be disbanded. One major urban university runs the second-
largest police force in its state, something as unheard-of in
Grandfather's day as it is demanded by anxious parents today.
Continue with psychological counselors, career counselors,
coaches for intercollegiate sports, and so on. It is extremely
easy to remove "administrators" wholesale, very difficult to do
so retail. And I have not mentioned the hosts of nonfaculty
academic support staff who man the labs and libraries and
fulfill government regulations demanded of the institution.

The proliferation of deans, counselors, and other student-
life professionals is a by-product of the underlying professionalization of university faculties. In the days of the classical
curriculum, faculty not only taught masterpieces of morality,
but they considered it their direct duty to enforce that morality.
The minutes of nineteenth-century faculty meetings are almost
completely given over to faculty sanctions against aberrant student behavior. At Princeton in the early 1960s—which was
not exactly before the Flood—the faculty solemnly (well, not

so solemnly) would vote as a body to punish students for "violations of the rules regarding women in the dormitories." After a while, nuclear physicists prefer to leave student naughtiness to others. In short, as faculties become professional scholars they cease playing amateur moralists.

It is, again, the *American* model of higher education that creates these costs. Just as the French have always found it bizarre that Americans bring legal action for "alienation of affections," so they find it equally odd that we house, feed, counsel, cajole, advise, and moralize our young in institutions of higher learning. The tradition that college is *more than* a mere education creates *more than* simple educational services and costs. Blame the high cost of tuition on the Pilgrims.

Admitting that there has been a real escalation of university costs, due, broadly speaking, to the professionalization of faculty, I end this excursion on cost with a comment on why college costs *seem* to have increased even beyond the small inroad on family disposable income.

I have often thought that the reason my father could afford to send me to college was that Yale University ran on direct current. The university in those days generated its own electricity and it was DC. Direct current is great for the family college budget because almost nothing will run on it. Anything with a constant-speed motor—electric clocks, electric razors, and so on—needs the cycle of alternating current to operate. Consider what one might save in the current day if students could not play (or buy) records or tapes. (I suspect I owned the only wind-up phonograph at Yale in my day.)

Before anyone starts a mass movement back to DC, I have to point out that science has progressed in the recent past, and what with transistors and all, anything runs on anything these days. And that is the point of my story. Part of the reason that college education seems to make such a dent in family disposable income is that there is just more there to dispose income upon. My father was saved buying me an electric clock by sheer fate; he did not have to worry about the cost of a TV set or computer. The American standard of living, measured by access to a variety of goods and services, has risen sharply since the meager days of World War II and its aftermath. The collegiate dollar today competes with a variety of highly attractive family options that just did not exist fifty years ago.

A second family story: My father-in-law was a farmer who, having lost one farm in the Depression, eked out a living on a small chicken ranch until World War II. Suddenly, chickens were worth real money. He was by nature an abstemious Swede, but even had he been a profligate there was nothing to spend money on during the war since all production was directed at the war effort. What he wanted was that his three children should have the benefit of a college education, and it was relatively easy to save money for that purpose, given his character and the conditions of the time. Collegegoing still cost a lot out of a farmer's income, but there just wasn't much else worthwhile for sale.

The irony of the collegegoing–versus–disposable cash dilemma is that one of the prime motivators for sending young people to college traditionally has been that they would advance economically in the society. And so they have. Having achieved—at least partly through advanced education—a greater income than Grandfather and Father, the contemporary beneficiary may feel cheated when funds that Mother hoped would buy the children a few luxuries are getting diverted back into education.

If college education costs a lot—even if it costs more than it used to on a proper scale—the issue of cost is finally a matter of what is valued and what is truly valuable. The grandparents saved every penny for education because they thought it was the best thing they could give to their children. It will come as no surprise to the reader that I consider higher education a life bargain even at twice the price.

Afterword

The one sure result of higher education is that students become alumni or alumnae. This entitles them to frame a diploma and receive requests for annual donations. For many years the University of Rochester purveyed a diploma approximately six inches by eight inches—surely a candidate for the *Guinness Book of World Records* in the exotic category of World's Smallest Diploma. As one alum said to me: "My dear departed father—what it cost him per square inch!" ($1500/sq.in. at current prices.) One of the clear triumphs of my administration has been to enlarge the diploma.

I began this book with the subject of cost—I end with it as well. What do we know about the value per square inch of college to alumni? There is no doubt, despite Ms. Bird, that college education is a route to better living. David Riesman years ago characterized college as the American rite of passage to the middle class. America is broad across the middle and it seems to make very little difference for class distinction whether the degree is from Ivy or State. It is being a college grad that makes the grade. Of course, not everyone in the middle class is upper-middle or upper-upper-middle income, but it is the subtle aroma of diploma that determines class, not income.

In his book *The Americans*, Daniel Boorstin notes that Americans have a peculiar tendency to congregate. For a nation of individualists we always seem to be on the lookout for something to join. His most amusing example is that after the income tax was introduced, Americans began to class themselves by certain tax brackets. Suddenly there were those in the upper income-tax brackets. The joiner tendency may also account for the idea of alumni. I believe that the alumni idea reflects a peculiar American sensibility. European universities have a sense of "old school connection" but it is not an *alumni* sense. A senior French executive at Schlumberger was explaining to me that he was doing business with a fellow graduate at L'École Normale Supérieure: "He knows because I am a *Normalien* and he is a *Normalien* that there are certain ways in business in which I will not screw him!" Fellow Harvardians do not have this French sense of *délicatesse*.

The American alumni sense is broader but thinner. One will gladly mellow out at a reunion with classmates, but business is business, after all. Alumni loyalty is not so much personal as institutional. Of course, many grads maintain collegiate friendships for life, and coeducation has been a boon to alumni marriages—at least in the days when marriage was a fashion. What is unusual is not friendship, then, but the fact that individuals retain a sense of alumnihood, a loyalty to Siwash. Alumni want the college's name to shine, the football team to excel, the president to be affable, and the students to behave. I may misconceive the exact sensibility of American alumni loyalty, but I am not wrong in pointing out that it is only in America that graduates offer financial support to their place of higher education. While charitable deductions for those upper-income tax brackets may be a partial cause, the astounding fact is that the collegiate years create a sentimental sense sufficient for generating cash flow.

Alumni loyalty, like so many other aspects of higher education discussed in this book, is rooted in the denominational past. It is not just that congregations were used to tithing and the habit carried forward to the denominational college; it was that college was a true *passage* in life. College became a center of determinate memory from which one marked off childhood and adulthood. Those raucous religious revivals of yesterday were often moments of permanent life conversion. Alumni return to college both literally and psychologically because something unique happened there. College (growing up) is relived "sacramentally" at every reunion.

One can wonder whether the newfangled scientific research university will generate the loyalty that "conversion" offered in the past. On the surface the prospect may not appear too promising. The intellectual excellence of "science" introduces a distance and austerity to the overall university experience. The moralistic college of yore went for the soul. Nevertheless, the college years remain pivotal in the transition from childhood to adult responsibility. The triumphs or traumas of college years can be powerful. Lots of things happen for the first time. Alumni may continue to return to a place of first love or first failure.

If the denominational college is gone, its ghost remains and is unlikely to be wholly exorcised even by the most advanced, rational, and diffident course of study. As the denominational college has declined, so have denominations themselves. It is clear that churches no longer command the position in society that they enjoyed in the nineteenth century. The rational university may turn aside from theology, but the university may be the sole institution in the country to enjoy both power and idealism. If Berkeley were really a public educational factory, why would students there be so insistent that it be the moral and political leader of the nation?

The idealism of universities is more than a whiff of incense left over from a churchly past; it is inherent in the enterprise. Aspiration to high ideals is the best legacy for students and the assurance of alumni allegiance. But are universities really after high ideals? Presidents proclaim that every commencement, but they also know the low politics and debilitating economic compromises that define much of daily life on the quad.

High ideals are inherent, essential, inescapable in the academy. I cannot imagine one day passing without a sensing of that fact. Several years ago I had the privilege of touring one of the major university accelerator facilities. Nothing could better instantiate the modern scientific research university than this mammoth instrument. Nothing might seem less humanistic. Nothing might seem likely to stir the heart of a loyal alum. For the life of me, however, I could think of no better metaphor for the place than a Trappist monastery. Monks rise at all hours to tend the highest mystery of being; scientists hovered at all hours in their experimental cubicles around the powerful mysteries of fundamental matter. The austerity of prayer was duplicated in the austere precision of the scientific observation. Monks and scientists want to know the truth at the heart of mystery. That is life dedication.

Not all of university life is as grandly displayed as a megavolt cyclotron—nor as expensive, thank goodness. Yet it is difficult to fancy anyone drifting through four years at anywhere from Lowly Branch U. on up the scale who is not struck by the *difficulty* of advanced learning. The lesson of this book has been the importance of faculty and their disciplines. Disciplines indeed. The difficulty creates the discipline. Discipline toward what is high and difficult is the university's best lesson.

Index